THE YEAR
IN TENNIS 2010

DAVIS CUP
by BNP PARIBAS

ITF
International Tennis Federation

Text by Clive White

The International Tennis Federation

Universe

First published in the United States of America in 2010 by

UNIVERSE PUBLISHING

A Division of Rizzoli International Publications, Inc.

300 Park Avenue South

New York, NY 10010

www.rizzoliusa.com

© 2010 by the International Tennis Federation

2011 2012 2013 / 10 9 8 7 6 5 4 3 2 1

Designed by Domino 4 Limited, Weybridge, United Kingdom
Printed in Italy

ISBN: 978-0-7893-2210-4

CONTENTS

President's Message

This year's Davis Cup by BNP Paribas produced some memorable stories, but none more so than the dramatic final in Belgrade that saw a new nation's name engraved on Dwight Davis's 110-year-old trophy.

For those lucky enough to see firsthand what winning the Davis Cup meant to the Serbian team, as well as the vociferous home supporters who filled the Belgrade Arena for three full days, it underlined the importance of this competition in the modern game.

Tennis might have changed dramatically since the first two-nation contest between the United States and the British Isles in 1900, but the ideals of fostering international understanding, representing one's country, and valuing teamwork in a sport usually associated with individual endeavor remain the same.

It takes two teams to create a classic Davis Cup tie like the one in Belgrade, and I'm sure I will not be alone in thanking France for playing its part in a thrilling finale to a wonderful year, but the plaudits must go to Serbia. Its rise to prominence in this competition has been rapid.

Serbia had not won a World Group tie before this year but overcame four former champions in the shape of the United States, Croatia, Czech Republic, and France to claim the greatest team prize in tennis for the first time.

The familiar quartet of Novak Djokovic, Janko Tipsarevic, Viktor Troicki, and Nenad Zimonjic played in every tie this year, and it was their team spirit that shone through in the victory and in the celebrations both on and off court after their famous win against France.

It was wonderful to see how much it meant to Serbia—both its players and its people—and once again reiterates what makes Davis Cup so special. Tennis is an individual sport, yet Davis Cup is a team competition, and this brings out a different side to the players: it adds to the pressure; it makes the highs higher and the lows lower.

In 2010, 536 players representing 125 countries across four continents took part in Davis Cup. Such is the global nature of the competition that the Web continues to be the perfect platform in which to showcase it. This year saw the relaunch of daviscup.com and copadavis.com in time for the final in Belgrade. More than two-and-a-half million people logged onto the websites during event weekends alone, and it is hoped that the new-look portals will give users a more comprehensive online experience, which will be supported by social media initiatives on Twitter, Facebook, and YouTube.

This year, we welcomed back Adecco to our family of sponsors. The Human Resources Solutions provider signed a new agreement as international sponsor that will last until 2013. We are also proud to have secured BNP Paribas as our title sponsor until 2016. Their commitment to tennis and their global reach makes them the ideal partner.

All that remains is for me to congratulate the author of this book, Clive White, who in his first year of chronicling the highlights of Davis Cup has done a fantastic job. I also cannot forget to thank the wonderful photographers, whose hard work has not only provided this book with some of the most stunning images in tennis, but also captured the spirit of this special competition on our websites and in our magazines.

Lastly, my congratulations go to Serbia for its remarkable achievement and also to the National Associations that have been involved throughout the year in staging the eighty-two ties. I look forward to next season and hope to see you in 2011.

Francesco Ricci Bitti
ITF President

BNP PARIBAS | The bank for a changing world

The love affair continues

According to the main criteria, BNP Paribas (www.bnpparibas.com) is one of the six strongest banks in the world. BNP Paribas places its abilities and its skills at the service of its clients in all of the countries in which it operates. It also places them at the service of its sports sponsorship. BNP Paribas has supported tennis since 1973, demonstrating its capacity to adapt through a policy based on warm and dynamic partnership. The relationship between BNP Paribas and tennis is mutually beneficial. It has been developed with care and loyalty to the sport in order to attain a worldwide reputation that reflects the qualities of the group's work in the field of banking.

Sports sponsorship at the service of the brand

The BNP Paribas brand is a major asset for the company in its contact with people across all areas of its activity. In it they see a human quality as it conveys emotional values and above all, acts as a familiar landmark in an increasingly globalized environment. The BNP Paribas brand system is a means of reconciling a strong international image with a local relationship. BNP Paribas has now become a powerful, innovative, warm, and cohesive international brand. Tennis sponsorship is one of the springboards used to spread its influence.

Tennis sponsorship at the service of the international deployment of the brand

BNP Paribas has gradually developed its partnership mechanism to accompany all aspects of the tennis boom: professional, family, educational, and social. From the year 2000 onward, the emphasis has been placed on developing tennis partnerships on an international basis in order to support the growth of the group's banking activities throughout the world. Thus sports sponsorship became the chosen means of supporting the development of the reputation of the BNP Paribas brand in countries where the group is established. This strategic choice initially took the form of Davis Cup sponsorship, which started in 2001. Step by step the structure was reinforced with support provided for the Monte Carlo Masters, the Internazionali BNL d'Italia in Rome and, most recently, the BNP Paribas Open in Indian Wells and the Shanghai Masters.

In the same way, the Group's values and social commitments are reflected in the further development of its sponsorship program, which includes:
- Support for women's sports through Fed Cup by BNP Paribas, the Bank of the West Classic tournament in California (WTA Tour), and the Strasbourg Women's International Tennis tournament
- Support for underprivileged youth through the "Fête le Mur" charity (created by Yannick Noah)
- Diversity through the Invacare World Team Cup and NEC Tour wheelchair events.

Our commitment is one of the longest in the history of the sport, just like the relationship the bank aims to develop every day with its clients, based on trust and reciprocity.

We are proud to be the title partner of Davis Cup and hope you will enjoy reliving the great moments of 2010 in this yearbook. We would like to congratulate all the teams that took part in the competition and in particular both the French and Serbian teams for the fantastic final they played in Belgrade. See you in 2011!

7 Pébereau

Michel Pébereau
Chairman, BNP Paribas

Foreword

It's no secret that winning the Davis Cup was a priority for me this year, and I can safely say that achieving that goal was the best feeling I have ever experienced in tennis. It was unbelievable.

Winning the Australian Open in 2008 was obviously a massive achievement for me, but winning Davis Cup is something else entirely. Tennis is an individual sport, and it is only in Davis Cup that we get to share the emotion and joy that come with a team victory.

And that's the point. This has not been an individual effort. All four of us have contributed in a big way to what can only be described as the biggest sporting prize our country has ever won. Viktor's performance in the fifth rubber against Michael Llodra showed the rest of the world just how good a player he is—something we have known for years.

Janko was brilliant in the semifinals against the Czech Republic, and Nenad has given so much to his country for the last sixteen years that there is no one on the team more deserving of this victory than him. Our captain, Bogdan, has been there every step of the way, and his belief in us as a group of players is contagious.

Let's not forget that the team that won Davis Cup this year was not just about the players—we have had wonderful support behind the scenes. We have to thank our fitness coaches, our physio, our stringer—everyone—for doing such a great job. The secret to our success has been friendship.

To win Davis Cup on home soil was extra special. I will never forget the atmosphere our fans created at the Belgrade Arena. The noise they made and the support they gave us will never be forgotten. I have to say that I was equally impressed by the traveling French supporters. They helped lift their players and really added to the sense of occasion.

And that's why I love this competition so much. I remember the first time I played Davis Cup. I was just sixteen years old, playing in a zonal tie against Latvia. It might not have been the most exciting match of my career, but to play for your country at such a young age was a brilliant feeling.

Three years later, I was part of the team that beat Australia to win Serbia's place in the World Group for the first time. I won the rubber against Chris Guccione that sealed our place in the top flight in front of a home crowd at the Belgrade Arena—it was another great memory that this competition has given me.

Winning one Davis Cup is a wonderful feeling, but now I want more. Playing with Viktor, Janko, and Nenad is like playing alongside your brothers. We have fun together on and off the court. I hope we will bring more success for Serbia in years to come, and I hope you will be there to enjoy it with us.

Novak Djokovic

The rise of Serbia

At the start of the year it was impossible to look past Spain as the Davis Cup champion for 2010. The same country had won it the two previous years; it possessed the best player in the world in Rafael Nadal (who was committed to it) and it had a strength in depth that made even France look a bit shallow. And yet there was an inescapable feeling that, as football managers are fond of saying, Serbia's name was on the old trophy.

There was certainly a strong feel-good factor about Serbia winning the title. Its rapid rise as a force in both men's and women's tennis these past four years or so has been one of those against-all-the-odds stories that the public adores. The bombing of Belgrade and Serbia's lack of money and facilities were captured perfectly by the media's story of a sweet, attractive young girl practicing in a disused swimming pool between Nato bombing raids.

In 2008 Novak Djokovic became the first Serb to win a Grand Slam singles title at the Australian Open, and then five months later that girl from the pool, Ana Ivanovic, took the plunge, winning the French Open to become No. 1 player in the world. Hollywood could not have written a better tearjerker.

So all that was needed for a happy ending to the story, or at least the ending to this particular chapter of it, was for Serbia to win the Davis Cup or Fed Cup. What chance had France, Spain, Argentina, and the rest against that gathering force of goodwill? Of course, Serbia needed the luck of the draw and a lot more besides to reach that zenith.

For example, who would have guessed that Spain, the champion four times during the 2000s, would not only lose to France, but lose 5–0? Even allowing for the fact that Nadal was absent with an injury—another stroke of luck for Bogdan Obradovic's side—it was an upset that was without precedent in Davis Cup competition. However, these things are never exactly what they seem, and even Guy Forget, the French captain, had to admit, prior to the final in Belgrade, that it was a tie in which "we could have won all the matches and we could have lost them."

On such knife edges do the fates of others turn, because Serbia—or any team for that matter—would not have wanted to face Spain, with or without Nadal. From the very first round the fates smiled benevolently on a young nation performing for only the fourth year in the competition under the flag of Serbia.

Whenever they wavered Djokovic was always there to pull them through. There was a single-mindedness about his approach to the Davis Cup that we hadn't seen before, a realization from early on that this could be Serbia's time, as he pointed out before the final.

"This is maybe the biggest occasion of our lives and we are aware of that," he said. "This is maybe one chance of the lifetime to have it at home and the support of the crowd will probably be crucial."

The twenty-three-year-old "Djoker" seemed to mature as a player as well as a person throughout the course of the season, and his defeat of Federer in the semifinals of the US Open was proof of that. He stopped his hilarious imitations of other players long ago, but fortunately he hasn't completely lost his sense of humor as anyone who saw him at the O2 Arena in November will realize when, after an incident with a contact lens in his group match against Nadal, he came out wearing an eye patch for the next one.

If the Serbs were unfortunate to draw the most successful nation in the history of the competition in the United States they, were doubly fortunate to get them at home (it was drawn by lots) and immediately after the retirement from Davis Cup of Andy Roddick and James Blake (only Blake's retirement is permanent). Roddick is the only player in the Top 10, apart from Nadal and Federer, who has a winning record against Djokovic (if, somewhat surprisingly, a losing one against the nominal Serbian No. 2, Janko Tipsarevic).

Similarly, in the quarterfinals, while they were again unfortunate to draw a side as redoubtable as neighbors Croatia away in their stronghold of Split, they were rather fortunate that Ivo Karlovic, the gentle giant who gives everyone trouble, had to withdraw on the eve of the tie because of injury, the Croats already having lost the services of Mario Ancic.

Against Czech Republic in the semifinals, Serbia could easily have been out of the competition by day two. The loss of Djokovic from the opening rubber against Radek Stepanek—ostensibly because of a dodgy tummy, but a combination of jet lag and fatigue from playing Nadal four days earlier in the final of the US Open cannot have helped—left them seemingly at the mercy of the previous year's runner-up.

However, Tipsarevic, as is his wont, made nonsense of a thirty-place discrepancy in the rankings to beat Berdych and square the tie, and then after Serbia lost the doubles Djokovic got off his sick bed—and the deck in the second set—to beat Berdych and thereby avenge his Wimbledon semifinal defeat to the same player two months earlier. Afterward, Tipsarevic completed what was anything but the formality of victory against Stepanek.

And so it went on right through to the happy ending in the final against France, for which home advantage was awarded to the Serbs on the basis that the last time the old country of Yugoslavia played the French, in 1991, the tie was held in Pau in the Pyrenees.

France had been without its No. 1, Jo-Wilfried Tsonga (who was 5–2 up in head-to-heads with Djokovic), since the first round, and now at a late stage it lost its new doubles specialist, Julien Benneteau, through injury. Again the Serbians found themselves on the back foot after day two, leaving Forget to remark: "I guess probably the captain is going to tell Novak and his boys tonight that the same thing could happen again, and it could very well do."

Keep their date with destiny they did, not to mention a promise that they would shave their heads if they won. It was nothing if not a close shave at times for Serbia.

"I think they were beyond what we expected," conceded Forget. "I think Serbia deserved to win because they were behind and they came back again. Obviously it's a great advantage to play at home. Probably if we would have played in Paris, somewhere else, things would have been, maybe, a little bit different."

As for Les Bleus, it was another magnificent effort, not least because it was produced for the most part without their strongman, Tsonga, who still turned up to act as cheerleader. Woe betide the rest of the world if they ever get him fit and playing regularly. Aside from 2009, they have made the quarterfinals or better every year since 2001.

France's players could be forgiven for thinking this was going to be their year when, after beating Germany 4–1 and thrashing Spain, they handed out another whitewash to no less a power than Argentina. If the French football team had produced a similar range of results at the South African World Cup, they would have come home in triumph instead of disgrace.

Argentina's David Nalbandian had been acquiring an aura of invincibility in the competition this year until he crossed forehands and backhands with Monfils on day one in Lyon and then suddenly a Davis Cup dream was over for another year for the twenty-eight-year-old. The truth is it was probably an away trip too far for Tito Vasquez's side after they had upset the formbook in Sweden and Russia.

At thirty years of age, Michael Llodra has even more reason to believe that this could have been his last chance of achieving the glory that all French players have dreamed of savoring since the days of the Four Musketeers. Elevated to the No. 2 spot in the absence of Tsonga, he, too, had an outstanding Davis Cup year, winning all six of his singles and doubles rubbers until he fell foul of an inspired Viktor Troicki in the one that mattered most. It would have taken a cold heart not to sympathize with him during a tearful aftermath.

The standard of this Davis Cup was extraordinarily high. With all due respect to Israel, who reached the semifinals in 2009, there is no way they could have made such progress in 2010. Of the eight quarterfinalists, only Chile came from outside the Top 10 and the likes of United States, Switzerland, and Sweden didn't even make it that far.

Spain retained its No. 1 ranking despite its premature elimination and went into the New Year still more than 6,000 points ahead of the new champion. You can be sure, as far as Albert Costa's side is concerned, Serbia has just borrowed the title for a year. ●

First Round 5–7 March

		Czech Republic defeated Belgium 4–1	BREE, BELGIUM—INDOOR CLAY
		France defeated Germany 4–1	TOULON, FRANCE—INDOOR HARD
		Russia defeated India 3–2	MOSCOW, RUSSIA—INDOOR HARD
		Chile defeated Israel 4–1	COQUIMBO, CHILE—OUTDOOR CLAY
		Serbia defeated USA 3–2	BELGRADE, SERBIA—INDOOR CLAY
		Spain defeated Switzerland 4–1	LOGRONO, SPAIN—INDOOR CLAY
		Argentina defeated Sweden 3–2	STOCKHOLM, SWEDEN—INDOOR HARD
		Croatia defeated Ecuador 5–0	VARAZDIN, CROATIA—INDOOR HARD

Introduction

The earthquake in Chile on the eve of a new Davis Cup by BNP Paribas season inevitably cast a shadow over the World Group first-round proceedings. While a substantial 4–1 victory by Chile against Israel in the delayed tie can hardly be said to have given the weekend a happy ending, it did remind everyone of the important part that sport has to play in the healing process during times of great tragedy.

Otherwise, the opening round was most notable for Serbia's historic victory against the United States, which put this fledgling nation—that had never played in the competition before 1995—into the quarterfinals for the first time. How appropriate that it was Novak Djokovic, Serbia's most famous tennis player, who led them to it in his hometown of Belgrade.

However, if it was possible to award an individual prize in what is unarguably one of the world's great team competitions it would have to go to David Nalbandian. The Argentine had barely hit a tennis ball in nine months because of injury, but at the last minute offered his much-needed services to his country, took a flight to Stockholm, and was instrumental in securing a narrow victory over Sweden.

The United States aside, all of the strongest nations survived their opening encounters. Defending champion Spain did so by beating Switzerland with virtually a reserve team, while France could afford to omit two recent top 10 players and still be too strong for Germany. Last year's runner-up, the Czech Republic, continued to put its faith in the two-man team of Radek Stepanek and Tomas Berdych against Belgium and was suitably rewarded.

As for countries like Russia and Croatia, the personnel may have changed but the end result—success—remained the same, as India and Ecuador discovered to its cost. Croatia, the champion in 2005, threatened to prevail again in 2010 with a completely different team. Serbia would have something to say about that in a quarterfinal tie that was eagerly awaited by the rest of the world, never mind the Balkans. ●

Belgium v Czech Republic

It's generally agreed that in order to be really successful at Davis Cup, a country needs two good singles players and at least one, if not two, doubles specialists. Czech Republic meets those requirements admirably but prefers to rely essentially upon just two men: Tomas Berdych and Radek Stepanek.

Whatever works best for you seems to be the criteria for some teams. After all, in 2005, Ivan Ljubicic won the Davis Cup virtually single-handedly. The balding, likeable Croat won eleven out of twelve rubbers, including doubles. It wasn't until the final against Slovak Republic that his sidekick, Mario Ancic, won a live singles rubber, and then it proved to be the most crucial of the lot—the fifth and final one.

Czech Republic's deadly twosome did their stuff again on the clay of the Bree Expodrome in eastern Belgium, beating the host nation as comfortably as the 4–1 scoreline might suggest. It takes a very good nation, such as Spain in last year's final, to beat them.

Five or six years ago that might have been Belgium too, but as a first-choice pairing Olivier Rochus and Xavier Malisse, both twenty-nine, are not the force they once were, although the diminutive Rochus continues to defy the years—and the quality of the opposition—with occasional bursts of excellence in tournament play, as he ended up showing at Miami when he surprised world No. 2 Novak Djokovic.

Over the years the tricky Rochus has often been a thorn in the side of big men, like Marat Safin and Ivo Karlovic, so he cannot have been without hope of toppling another goliath of the modern game in the six-foot, five-inch Berdych in the opening rubber. After all, he had beaten him in their first two meetings on clay. But Berdych is a more complete player these days and had won their last two meetings on the surface.

Rochus was in trouble from the start, and it was four games before the Belgian crowd, which was regularly out-roared by the small Czech contingent, had something to cheer about. If the first set slipped away from him all too easily, it was nothing compared to the speed with which Rochus lost the second set after the crushing disappointment of failing to convert any of six break points in the second game. When a let ball handed Berdych a 4–0 lead, Rochus must have known a bagel was heading his way.

Just as in the previous two sets, Rochus fatally dropped serve at the start of the third, and Berdych sped away to a 6–3 6–0 6–4 victory. "I felt pretty good out there," said Rochus somewhat surprisingly,

"but Tomas played an excellent match. He's not No. 25 in the world for nothing."

Like Rochus, Malisse would have harbored hopes of a victory in the second rubber, having beaten his opponent Stepanek in straight sets only a month earlier in San Jose. But when it comes to Davis Cup, Stepanek is a different animal, and he quickly imposed himself upon the Belgian, whose best chance of getting a foothold in the game came at 1–1 in the second set when a backhand error by the Czech gave Belgium its first break of the tie.

But Stepanek immediately broke back, and the next time Malisse faced a break point it proved calamitous, a carelessly played slice giving Stepanek the second set. Malisse made a decent fist of it in the third, and with four consecutive breaks of serve the set could obviously have gone either way. It eventually went to a tiebreak, which Stepanek secured with two match points to spare, winning 6–2 6–4 7–6(3).

Czech Republic's Lukas Dlouhy is one of the best doubles players in the world, but Jaroslav Navratil, the captain, will invariably go with Stepanek and Berdych for the doubles unless either is injured or exhausted from the first day's play. That certainly wasn't the case here, so Stepanek and Berdych faced Olivier Rochus and Steve Darcis on day two. Darcis had been the hero

when Belgium beat Ukraine in the 2009 play-offs, winning both his singles rubbers, but he was up against a completely different quality of opponent here.

However, it was Rochus who was first broken at 3–3 in the first set. Berdych then dropped serve when serving for the set, only for the Czechs to win the eventual tiebreak without conceding a point. It was a precursor of what was to come. In the second set the Belgians had a hellish time, losing 6–0. When Rochus was broken again in the third set for Czech Republic to lead 3–1, the game was up for Belgium in more ways than one, and Berdych eventually served out the match 7–6(0) 6–0 6–3.

Darcis eventually secured a consolation point for the Belgians when he beat Jan Hajek 7–6(6) 1–6 6–4 at the start of day three before Dlouhy eventually got to hit a ball, beating Christophe Rochus 1–6 7–6(3) 7–5.

"I still can't believe how great the guys played this weekend," said Navratil of his 2009 runners-up. "With a team like this I am confident against any nation." ●

Pictured above from left:
Captain Jaroslav Navratil
and Tomas Berdych (CZE);
Xavier Malisse (BEL)
Pictured below:
Steve Darcis (BEL)

France v Germany

One look at France's bench told you all you needed to know about the likely outcome of its first-round tie against Germany: Gilles Simon and Richard Gasquet, two players who were in the top 10 a year or two ago, were seated there—when they weren't jumping up and down to support their teammates—from the first rubber until the last. It's the kind of "redundancy" all countries need if they want to win the Davis Cup.

There was a time when the name "Becker" in the opposition's ranks would have had France cowering. Fortunately for the French, they only had to deal with that particular Becker on one occasion, and that was in a doubles rubber in 1996 when the great man was past his best.

another victory in 2001. Although the country's No. 2, Gael Monfils, spoke before this tie of how it was "traditional" for France to win Dwight Davis's old trophy, it hasn't done so again since then.

This time Forget did not repeat the mistake he made at the same stage of last year's competition, when he spoke of his team in the same breath as the Four Musketeers—Jean Borotra, Henri Cochet, Rene Lacoste, and Jacques Brugnon—before losing 3–2 to Czech Republic. But he could happily have risked another mention of the famous quartet this time, because it was sixty-two years since Germany beat France and forty-seven years since they won a live rubber against the French team.

Pictured clockwise from top:
Gael Monfils (FRA);
The opening ceremony in Toulon;
Benjamin Becker (GER)

Guy Forget was on the opposite side of the net that day to help clinch a quarterfinal victory in two days for France. Now as captain, he watched from the sidelines as his team diffused the somewhat less potent threat of Benjamin Becker and company in equally quick time. With Germany unable to call upon the services of the injured Tommy Haas and Nicolas Kiefer, an unassailable 3–0 win reflected the gulf in class between the two countries. Then again, Germany had also lost in two days last time, in 2006, when both Haas and Kiefer played.

In 1996 France had gone on to win the Davis Cup for an eighth time, and Forget, as captain, led them to

Both teams had more than ten players in the top 100 this particular week, but Germany's highest-ranked player present, Philipp Kohlschreiber, was ranked only 30, while three in the French team were ranked higher. Furthermore, several Germans declared themselves unavailable. As a result, the French esprit de corps seemed greater, as was exemplified by the determined way they performed in the dead rubbers, and the capacity crowd in Toulon.

It's not difficult to see why France has been so successful at Davis Cup. The country is totally committed to it, and that passion for the competition

is handed down from generation to generation. "For me it's difficult to understand all the people who don't play this competition," said France's No. 1, Jo-Wilfried Tsonga, who was just fifteen when France last won the cup. "It's maybe the best competition in tennis. For me it's really important because you represent your country and you have to honor it."

Tsonga, like his three French teammates, resides just across the border in Switzerland, which made them an ideal target for French television's *Action Discrète* program. Dressed up in Swiss flags, members of the production team turned up at the

draw to ask the French team if, in the absence of Roger Federer, they could be adopted as the new Swiss team. One member of the cast took the stunt a little too far and was evicted for rowdy behavior, but the French players saw the funny side of it even if they rejected the offer.

Although gale force winds were wreaking havoc in Toulon, Patrik Kuhnen, the German captain, knew that his team needed to get off to a serene start on the indoor hard court at the Palais des Sports if they were to have any chance of running the French ship aground. While he got one half of his wish, which was that Kohlschreiber, his No. 1, played first, the second half of it—that he raised his game as he has done before for important matches—never materialized.

When Germany faced Spain, the defending champion, in Marbella in the previous year's quarterfinal, Kohlschreiber unexpectedly won both his singles rubbers against the higher-ranked Fernando Verdasco and Tommy Robredo, and in fact, had won his previous four rubbers.

Kohlschreiber's opponent Monfils, on the other hand, had only ever played one singles rubber before, against the Dutchman Thiemo de Bakker the previous September, which he lost. He had missed the tie against Czech Republic after traveling to Acapulco, so this year he gave the Mexican tournament a miss and felt the better for it. But he still declared himself only "85 percent" confident in his game despite avenging

gastro illness that had caused him to lose seven pounds. No such luck. The slim-line version of Tsonga proved just as awesome as the full-weight one as he defeated Becker 6–3 6–2 6–7(2) 6–3. Both men's Davis Cup records were nothing if not uniform: Tsonga had now played seven, won seven; Becker played three, lost three.

So it went to the doubles and Germany's final hope of upsetting the form book with their pairing of Kohlschreiber and Christopher Kas. Michael Llodra and Julien Benneteau had arrived straight from winning the doubles event at the Marseille tournament just along the coastal road, and the bad news for the Germans was that it was soon obvious that they would be continuing the long history of French success in this event.

The French pair, according to Kohlschreiber, "came out like a hurricane," and blew them away. Llodra was playing his seventeenth Davis Cup doubles, Benneteau his first. In fact, it was Benneteau's Davis Cup debut, which was surprising for someone so highly ranked but an indication of how blessed the French are for talent. Llodra, naturally, was the driving force in a 6–1 6–4 1–6 7–5 win.

Kohlschreiber gave credit where it was due. "The French team is not seeded—it's No. 9 in the world— but they have such good players it's like a fake number. They should be much higher ranked," he said. ●

that defeat to de Bakker three weeks earlier in Rotterdam. It wasn't long, though, before he raised his confidence level that further 15 percent.

That was partly due to the fact that Kohlschreiber struggled with his first serve throughout and got very few cheap points on it, unlike Monfils, who started with an ace and carried on from there. When it was pointed out to the German No. 1 that he didn't seem to be moving as well as the athletic Monfils, he had an amusing explanation for it. "If you see him moving on the other side [of the net] everybody looks like a turtle."

This was one "turtle" who was out of its depth and soon sunk, losing 6–1 6–4 7–6(5). Now the Germans were banking on Tsonga still showing the after-effects of a

Russia v India

Anyone who can come from two sets down to clinch a heroic victory in the fifth and final rubber of a Davis Cup final can never be said to live in the shadow of others. But Mikhail Youzhny, more often than not, has had to occupy a backseat in the Russian drive toward a position of preeminence in the game. Then again, so have most Russian men. But with the larger-than-life Marat Safin retired and the underrated Nikolay Davydenko injured, the first-round tie against India presented Youzhny with the opportunity to steal the limelight, which he did in his own inimitable, modest manner.

The withdrawal one hour before the first day's opening rubber of the Russian No. 2, Igor Andreev, with a knee injury (there is no truth in the rumour that he did it during their traditional pre-tie kickabout) also put some

pressure on him. But he rose to the challenge just as we knew Youzhny would to give Russia a commanding lead that never looked like it would be relinquished.

Youzhny was just twenty years of age—as was his opponent Paul-Henri Mathieu in that 2002 final—when he was asked to deliver a victory in front of a fiercely partisan Paris crowd, not for himself but for his country, on a day they had awaited for forty years. If ever a match summed up what Davis Cup is all about it was that one. Youzhny's breathtaking victory from a seemingly hopeless position will live with him forever, just as defeat will probably live with the unfortunate Mathieu.

The opening rubber here in the Small Sports Arena Luzhniki in Moscow was not one of those defining moments in a player's career, but it was pretty important to the outcome of this tie. Somdev

Devvarman, the Indian No. 1, was a point away from a two-sets-to-love lead when Igor Kunitsyn just managed to hold before doing a "Youzhny."

Had India won this opening rubber it would have made the tie very interesting for two reasons. One, its renowned doubles partnership of Leander Paes and Mahesh Bhupathi would have given India the lead going into the final day's play instead of just reducing the arrears. And two, Russia might have allowed the memory of the previous year's embarrassing 4–1 quarterfinal defeat to Israel to play on its mind. After all, this was a weaker Russian team than it was then, and India was not so inferior to Israel. On top of that, Youzhny was nursing a back injury.

Kunitsyn was not the only one to be surprised by his late promotion from cheerleader to lead-off man. Andreev himself had not expected the call that he received while staying in Acapulco to practice for the upcoming Indian Wells Masters tournament. He was happy to make the long journey back home but probably had regrets about it when he injured his knee in training the night before the opening day's singles.

Shamil Tarpischev's team must have been the tiniest bit edgy beforehand and no doubt became increasingly so as Devvarman's safety-first tactics produced dividends. Kunitsyn had the reassurance of

knowing he had beaten his opponent comfortably in both their previous matches, but he was soon taken aback by the progress in Devvarman's game.

According to the Indian captain, Shiv-Prakash Misra, "Our boys play much better in Davis Cup than they do in an individual capacity." Evidence of that was Devvarman's sizeable comeback to earn India its first World Group tie in twelve years, when he came from two sets and a break down to beat South Africa's Rik de Voest in the decisive fourth rubber of the previous year's play-off in Johannesburg.

Leading 5–2 in the second set, he said he had Kunitsyn "where I wanted him," but he couldn't close out the set, and as the Russian, to his credit, kept attacking, the mistakes began to creep into Devvarman's game. When a controversial line call went Kunitsyn's way in the eighth game of the third set, he immediately capitalized on it by holding serve to take the set and went on to win 6–7(6) 7–6(4) 6–3 6–4.

"It's the first time I ever opened a Davis Cup tie for Russia, the first time I ever played a live singles match— it was a day of firsts for me," said a delighted Kunitsyn.

Rohan Bopanna started well enough in the second rubber and forced three break points to Youzhny's one in the first set, but predictably it was the Russian who converted his. A discrepancy of more than four hundred

Pictured clockwise
from top left:
Igor Kunitsyn (RUS) and
Somdev Devvarman (IND);
The doubles rubber;
Leander Paes (IND)
and daughter Anaiyha

places in the rankings meant someone even as experienced as Bopanna, who has been playing Davis Cup for nine years, had little chance, and the man who had just reached successive finals in Rotterdam and Dubai ran out a 6–4 6–2 6–3 winner in one hour and forty minutes.

At least a point for India in the doubles was a foregone conclusion. There was a wonderful throwaway remark from Paes before the tie when he said, "We know we're playing for 1.3 billion people." No pressure. Paes and Bhupathi are the most successful pairing in Indian Davis Cup history—the Amritraj brothers, Vijay and Anand, don't even come close—and though they no longer play together in tournaments they have clearly not lost their chemistry. "For us it's about keeping it special," said Paes, who was a Grand Slam champion with Lukas Dlouhy at both the French Open and US Open in 2009.

When the draw was made, he expected an "unorthodox" challenge from a team that is usually reliant on excellent singles players, like Safin, Davydenko, and Dmitry Tursunov. The untried pairing of Kunitsyn and Teimuraz Gabashvili never stood a chance and lost 6–3 6–2 6–2 in just one hour and thirty-five minutes. They were given more of a runaround than the Russian baddies in *Octopussy* when Vijay was famously in tandem with James Bond.

Gabashvili said he had played many of the top pairings, including Nenad Zimonjic and Daniel Nestor,

but thought the Indian pair superior. Kunitsyn even went as far as to rate Paes as "maybe the best volleyer in the game" and described Bhupathi's returning as "unbelievable." Be that as it may, Tarpischev knows he will need to come up with a better combination in future.

It was the Indian twosome's twenty-third consecutive Davis Cup victory stretching back to 1997, which Paes joked ought to qualify them for a place in the *Guinness World Records* book. When he arrived in Moscow, he said he was wearing five layers of clothing to protect him from the Russian winter, which, in fact, was much milder than normal. But there was never any danger of him catching a cold in this rubber.

The tie, as expected, was settled in the opening rubber on day three when Devvarman, by his own admission, was "completely outclassed" by Youzhny. His defensive tactics were mistaken against a player of such quality, and he only opened up when it was too late, his frustration boiling over into a bit of racquet-throwing as he lost 6–2 6–1 6–3. This gave Russia its seventeenth consecutive win at home and sixty-two-year-old birthday boy Tarpischev his forty-ninth victory as captain in a career stretching back to 1974. But as Bopanna made light of a three-hundred-place discrepancy in the rankings to beat Gabashvili 7–6(5) 6–4 in the dead rubber, India was left to ponder, "what if?" ●

Chile v Israel

Everything pales into insignificance after something as devastating as an earthquake, and to some it may seem disrespectful for sporting events to continue at a time of great tragedy, but sport can play its part in the healing process. Therefore, it was important that the Davis Cup tie between Chile and Israel went ahead despite its many obstacles, and Fernando Gonzalez and his teammates were gratified by how much it meant to the nation.

Gonzalez and Nicolas Massu had brought great pride and happiness to the country when they unexpectedly won their gold medals at the 2004 Athens Olympics in both the doubles and singles, and they must have felt it was their duty to deliver again in this Davis Cup World Group tie. "We will try to win and create some happiness for our country, for our people, in these difficult times," said Gonzalez. "I am saddened for what we are living as a country, but I am hopeful because we are a supportive, strong country. I am fully aware of what happened in Concepcion, in Talca, and I

am sending a message of hope: what doesn't kill you makes you stronger. Even Roger Federer messaged me, very worried. We are all very sensitive about this."

The earthquake that struck central and southern Chile on the weekend before the tie, measuring 8.8 on the Richter scale, was felt only as a soft tremor in Coquimbo, the venue for the tie, which is five hundred kilometers north of the capital, Santiago. But transportation issues led to the late arrival of players and officials, causing the tie to be delayed twenty-four hours.

Coquimbo is a traditional seaside holiday retreat for Chileans with a seventeen-kilometer beachfront and lots of night life during the summer. But there was now a strange tranquillity about the place as local people experienced mixed feelings of relief that their own city had been spared any harm and concern for fellow countrymen and women who were less fortunate. "Our thoughts and prayers are with the people of Chile," said Francesco Ricci Bitti, the president of the International Tennis Federation. "Dwight Davis founded Davis Cup to

foster international understanding between nations through tennis. We hope that this tie will fulfill this aim and help to start the healing process for the nation."

Needless to say, the ramifications of the draw were of minor consequence to the players. Afterward, players from both teams made a collection from people they knew (team members, television commentators, etc.) and raised, in about ten minutes, $2,000. With it they bought a truckload of goods, including food and hygiene products, and delivered it to the local office of a large relief organization, to be sent to the affected people in the south of Chile.

surprised everyone by reaching the semifinals the previous year, beating Sweden and Russia en route, and it took an excellent Spanish team to stop them in Murcia.

Dudi Sela, Israel's No. 1, was higher ranked than Massu, whom he had beaten in four sets in their only previous encounter two and a half years earlier when Israel defeated Chile in a World Group play-off match at Ramat Hasharon. But that was on a hard court, and Massu is a much more accomplished clay-court player. Nevertheless, it was Sela who started the better. After being broken in the opening game, he broke Massu three times to take the first set.

"It is hard to put yourself in the place of the people who have lost relatives or are having a rough time, but I think Chile is a wonderful country," said Massu. "When natural disasters strike, Chileans always lend a hand to their fellow man in trouble. It does not seem easy to focus on the match, but at the same time we will do our part to give our country a morale boost by winning this tie."

Of course, it was a particularly difficult tie for the Israeli players, as the last thing they wanted was to inflict more misery upon Chile. They showed great sensitivity. "Our hearts and thoughts are with the Chilean people," said Eyal Ran, the captain. "That said, once we go into the court we will do our best to win the matches."

Although they were the underdogs, they were confident of putting up a good show. After all, they had

Each of the rubbers during their 2007 meeting had lasted four to five hours, and it looked as if this tie might follow suit when Massu took the second set to level. The Chilean likes nothing better than wars of attrition, but this match soon began to go comfortably his way, and he won it 4–6 6–2 6–2 6–4, whereupon he held his younger brother Stefano in an intense embrace. "He is always traveling with me, enjoys my victories, and suffers with my defeats," said Massu.

Gonzalez was a much clearer favorite to win against Harel Levy, ranked 108 places beneath him, but he, too, was slowly into his stride, dropping the first set. Gonzalez had been the last of the players to arrive in Coquimbo, and when he did he spent some time supporting relief efforts. That may

Pictured clockwise
from top left:
Andy Ram (ISR) and
Jonathan Erlich (ISR);
Chile's victory lap;
Israeli fan
Pictured opposite:
Fernando Gonzalez (CHI)

or may not have affected his focus, but he was
in a lethargic mood initially whereas Levy played
above himself.

However, having missed the 2009 Davis Cup
season, Gonzalez was anxious to make amends and
slowly he took control of the match. Without raising his
game to the level of the top 10 player he is, he broke
Levy just once in each of the following three sets to win
2–6 6–3 6–4 6–4 and put Chile firmly in control.

Hans Gildemeister, the Chilean captain, chose to
rest Gonzalez and Massu in the doubles, but if anyone
thought that was tantamount to handing Israel a
point—their doubles specialists Jonathan Erlich and
Andy Ram had just won the Australian Open—they
were much surprised. Chile's rookie pair, Paul

Capdeville and debutant Jorge Aguilar, put up an
inspired performance, and it took all the know-how of
one of the world's best doubles teams to win 6–7(5)
7–6(9) 2–6 6–1 6–0. Nevertheless, it was a bizarre
finish given that the Chileans were on the brink of
an extraordinary victory when, with the conditions
quickening in the warmer weather, they lost twelve
of the last thirteen games.

Gonzalez had needed the rest; the fact that he
sat through the after-match press conference on the
Friday with ice bags on both knees was proof of that.
Israel was optimistic that Sela, "our magician," as
Ram called him, could conjure a repeat of the victory
he scored against Gonzalez in five sets during the
previous tie between the two countries. However,
Gonzalez had twice avenged that defeat in straights
sets and he was not about to get it wrong this time
either. Looking a class above his opponent, he won
6–4 6–4 6–3 to put Chile into the quarterfinals.

Smiling for the first time in the week, Gonzalez
said: "The important thing was to win, whichever
the way. We are very happy with this victory, and
we hope it is something to get happy about, even if
it's a small happiness, for all the people affected by
the earthquake."

It was only fitting that Aguilar, who was so
despondent about missing out on a famous victory
in his first Davis Cup tie in the doubles, should win
the dead rubber, beating Levy 7–6(3) 6–1. ●

Serbia v USA

The Serbian tennis phenomenon has been well documented, but only when it pulls off a victory like this one in the name of the country does one fully appreciate how far it has come in so short a time. Serbia had never even played Davis Cup before 1995 and has only resided in the World Group since 2008. Now it had beaten the most successful country in the history of Davis Cup.

Of course, this was not the United States team of the previous year, less still the team that won the Davis Cup three years prior: Andy Roddick and James Blake, the mainstays of the team, had retired from the competition after nine years' service to concentrate on their singles careers. But even with Roddick and Blake on board the team would have been hard pressed to survive this first-round tie on the clay in Belgrade.

The Bryan brothers, who now took on the role of team leaders, had no doubt what lay in store for them in Serbia—or "Disturbia" as they called it. Anyway, it was about time the Serbs had a home tie after first-round matches away against Spain and Russia in recent years. They were unlikely to get the benefit of home comforts too often again in this year's competition. As it turned out, the reception at the imposing Beogradska Arena was a little less hostile than the Americans had feared and in marked contrast to the very welcoming one they received at the official dinner on the eve of the tie.

If the name of Novak Djokovic, the world No. 2, had been uppermost in the American team's minds beforehand, it was burned into their consciousness by the end of the evening at Novak Café-Restaurant, where everything, from the cutlery to the bottled water, carried the "Novak" motif. You might say Serbia's most famous tennis player had them eating out of his hands before the tie had even begun.

The American team had big shoes to fill, but then the replacements, John Isner and Sam Querrey, are both big lads, as Andrew Jarrett, the Wimbledon referee, knows only too well. At a cocktail reception given by the U.S. ambassador, to which both teams and their families were invited, Jarrett approached one very tall gentleman and said: "I would assume you are John Isner's father?" The man replied: "Well, actually not, I'm Sam Querrey's father." Easily done, as was the mistake made by Querrey Sr., who later asked Jarrett: "Do you do a lot of refereeing?"

Pictured from left:

Novak Djokovic (SRB);

Sam Querrey (USA);

Belgrade Arena

Pictured clockwise
from top left:
Bob Bryan (USA) leads
the U.S. cheering squad;
Captain Bogdan Obradovic
(SRB) and his team;
Viktor Troicki (SRB)

For Bogdan Obradovic, the Serbian captain, differentiating between Viktor Troicki and Janko Tipsarevic for the second singles berth was even harder: in the world rankings they were immediately alongside one another at No. 35 and 36 respectively. But in the end Obradovic plumped for the former, who would open against Davis Cup debutant Isner.

It proved to be an inspired decision. Mike Bryan had predicted that the doubles rubber, which pitted himself and brother Bob against Nenad Zimonjic and Tipsarevic, could be the "swing point," but as it turned out this opening rubber may have decided the outcome of the tie.

Both camps knew the first set would be important, particularly to the Americans, as Isner is a good front runner. He may also be a gentle giant, but he is pretty ruthless when serving for a set. Somehow, though, he allowed the opportunity to slip from his grasp on this occasion, not to mention a 5–3 lead, and ended up dropping the set in a tiebreak. His captain, Patrick McEnroe, thought he started with "maybe a little too much adrenalin."

Isner hit back to win the second set also on a tiebreak, which only reminded him how close he had come to taking a commanding lead. Troicki was understandably a little nervous at the start, but once he got into the swing of things he took control and finished a deserving 7–6(4) 6–7(5) 7–5 6–4 winner. Poor Isner took the defeat harder than he might have if it were a tournament.

"This hurts," he said. "You don't want to let your team down—not that I did. I know I fought as hard as I could. I know what it's like to play a team sport, and whenever you lose you feel like you're not pulling your weight, so it's a disappointment, and the team's in a hole because of me."

That hole would soon get a lot deeper. Djokovic had beaten Querrey twice before, including once on clay in straight sets at Monte Carlo, and was fresh from winning the Dubai tournament. The first two sets were straightforward enough, both in Djokovic's favor, but Querrey got back into it in the third. Then he played a few loose shots at the start of the fourth, and before he knew it had lost the rubber 6–2 7–6(4) 2–6 6–3.

While certainly vociferous, the crowd wasn't as enthusiastic as Obradovic would have liked, for which he blamed a saturation of tennis on television; it made them a bit blasé, he thought. The doubles rubber should have ignited their passion because it promised to be close. The Bryan brothers' reputation of course was legendary, and they were unbeaten on clay in Davis Cup,

but Obradovic hoped that the Serbian pair, one a world-class doubles player, the other a very fine singles player, would present them with an unusual challenge.

As it turned out, the only challenge was to Mike Bryan's digestive system, which, on the morning of the match, conceded defeat to food poisoning. He was replaced by Isner. This would be the first time that Bob had played doubles with someone other than his brother at tour level, while the withdrawal cost Mike the chance to equal John McEnroe's streak of twenty consecutive Davis Cup ties. But if the Serbians thought that the outcome was a formality, they were much surprised as Bob Bryan and Isner pulled off a stirring 7–6(8) 5–7 7–6(8) 6–3 win over Zimonjic and Tipsarevic. And, in true Bryan fashion, they celebrated their win with a chest bump.

"Mike got room service—chicken curry—and at 3 a.m. he started to get the shakes and started to vomit. We put him on an IV, he came out to the stadium and tried to practice, but shook his head as he knew he couldn't finish a match," Bob Bryan said. "I picked John because I wanted to back up that big serve, and I think we combined pretty well."

So as originally expected the match went down to the third and final day. Having remarked how Querrey moved better on this surface than Isner and was better from the baseline, Djokovic must have been quietly

confident. But Isner was on a high after his doubles victory, if not a little fatigued, and he almost gave Djokovic the fright of his life. The Serbian eventually prevailed only on his sixth match point, with a score of 7–5 3–6 6–3 6–7(6) 6–4 in four and a quarter hours.

A victory for Querrey in the dead rubber by 7–5 6–2 against Troicki put a better complexion on the score line from the Americans' point of view, but there was no doubting which team deserved to win. It was a famous victory that put Serbia into the quarterfinals for the first time in its history, and Djokovic for one was suitably moved by it. "When you have this opportunity to play for your country and feel the team spirit, it's something you cannot describe with words," he said. ●

Spain v Switzerland

Injury put the first Roger v Rafa showdown in Davis Cup on hold for another year, and maybe it was fitting that it should be kept for a later, more crucial stage of the competition. This meant that the odds were stacked heavily against a Swiss victory, because Spain's strength in depth is so much greater. In fact, it's absurdly good.

What other team at any time in any era could be without its No. 1, 2, and 3 players and still be favorites to win a World Group tie? Not to mention favorites to win any tie, even a third consecutive final this year. If the Real Madrid of Zinedine Zidane days were the Galacticos of football, then the Spain of Rafael Nadal days are the Galacticos of tennis.

In fact, in addition to being without its three first-choice players—Nadal, Fernando Verdasco, and Juan Carlos Ferrero—Spain was also missing Feliciano Lopez. (Someone like Albert Montanes, ranked just outside the top 30, doesn't even get a look in). In their place, Albert Costa, the captain, called upon the services of David Ferrer, Nicolas Almagro, Tommy Robredo, and Marcel Granollers. Some reserve team.

The match was played in a converted bullring— the Plaza de Toros de la Ribera, replete with glass roof—in Logrono, the heart of the Rioja region. Costa's team couldn't have asked for a more Spanish setting had Placido Domingo entertained the crowd during

changeovers. As for Switzerland, it came into the match knowing that its substitute No. 1, Stanislas Wawrinka, was as rusty as the orange clay; he hadn't played a competitive match in six weeks while awaiting the birth of his first child.

It was not so much an uphill task that Switzerland faced as an attempt to scale Mont Blanc in flippers. But once Wawrinka had attached his crampons, the Swiss put up a very creditable challenge over the course of the three days. Needless to say, they were heavily dependent upon Wawrinka; indeed some would say overdependent. If the Swiss were to keep alive the illusion that they were here to win, it was imperative that Wawrinka take the opening rubber against Almagro.

Not surprisingly, that famous Swiss timing was a bit awry at the start, with the Spaniard forcing nine break points before his opponent got his first. The concerned Swiss captain, Severin Luthi, was never off his feet then, exhorting his charge, the white Swiss cross on the back of his red tracksuit making one think more of first aid than the national emblem. But slowly Wawrinka came to grips with the situation, and in the end his greater experience—Almagro was playing his first Davis Cup match on Spanish soil—probably proved decisive.

There was nothing much wrong with his timing when he requested a toilet break at 6–5 up in the fourth, shortly before squaring the match.

And although a break down in the final set, Wawrinka turned it around to win 3–6 6–4 3–6 7–5 6–3 in one minute short of four hours. It was a mature performance, as one might expect from someone who had just assumed the duties of fatherhood.

Costa would have preferred that Ferrer had been drawn first, then "Nico [Almagro] could play with one-zero up." His confidence wasn't misplaced. Ferrer raced through the first set of the second rubber against Marco Chiudinelli before it dawned on the 56th-ranked opponent that he had beaten the fellow on the other side of the net the last time they met, albeit three years previous in a dead rubber in Geneva. The big-hitting young Swiss suddenly began lashing out and roared into a 4–1 lead, giving rise to even grander hopes in the Swiss camp.

Ferrer, ranked 40 places above his rival, gradually pegged him back with the help of not a few double faults—"I must have made close to ten in that second set and that's usually my strength," said a disappointed Chiudinelli afterward. The Swiss again led 5–3 in the tiebreak, but Ferrer's fabled doggedness gradually wore him down before the Spaniard romped away with the third set to win 6–2 7–6(5) 6–1.

By Spain's standards, it was scratching the bottom of the rioja barrel by pairing Robredo with the Davis Cup debutant Granollers in the doubles. Yet while it was the first time they had played together in Davis Cup, they were quite familiar with one another as a pairing, having reached the final of the Paris Masters the previous November. And as it turned out they were too good for Wawrinka and Yves Allegro, winning 7–6(8) 6–2 4–6 6–4. Nevertheless, the Swiss pair were not without their chances, and the outcome might have been different had they not allowed three set points to slip through their fingers in the first-set tiebreak.

Wawrinka was not at his best and knew he had to rediscover that winning knack against Ferrer if Switzerland was to take this tie to the fifth and final rubber. More important, he needed to recharge his batteries pretty quick. His Spanish opponent, who had won their three previous meetings, had had his feet up, figuratively speaking, while Wawrinka was toiling toward his seventh hour on court in two days.

In the event, frustration and fatigue combined to overtake Wawrinka as much as his opponent. He seemed to be taking charge of the match in the second set when he suddenly allowed a few poor shots and a point deduction for racket abuse at a critical stage of the set to get to him. It seemed to break his resolve, and he ended up losing the last eleven games as well as the tie, which Ferrer won 6–2 6–4 6–0.

The Swiss captain was accused of asking too much of Wawrinka in his present physical condition by having him play three matches in three days, but he had no other option. If Switzerland was to make the most of its opportunity it had to win the tie over the first four rubbers, because the Swiss No. 3, Chiudinelli, as game as he is, could not be expected to beat the likes of Almagro on clay in a decisive rubber. Nor did he in the dead one, losing 6–1 6–3. ●

Sweden v Argentina

When David Nalbandian reached the 2002 Wimbledon final, losing to Lleyton Hewitt in straight sets, he was seen as a one-slam wonder, and that is what so far he has proved to be, but not because he isn't good enough to win a slam. There is surely no more enigmatic an individual in tennis than the powerfully built Argentine. At his best he is capable of beating any player in the world, and of winning any tournament. At his worst, well, he might just as well not turn up.

Just to make him even more difficult to fathom, he demonstrated in Sweden that when his spirit is willing, even when his flesh is weak, he is capable of extraordinary levels of achievement, which include single-handedly turning certain Davis Cup defeat into victory.

Argentina traveled to snow-covered Stockholm with about as much hope of beating Sweden at tennis as they would have at ice hockey. Without Juan Martin del Potro, Juan Monaco, Nalbandian, and a recognized doubles pairing, Tito Vazquez, their genial captain, must have feared an embarrassing reverse at the Kungliga Tennishallen, home of the Swedish Open and the scene of so many great Davis Cup triumphs during the days of Bjorn Borg.

Then two days before the event Vazquez got a call from Nalbandian to say he thought he might be fit enough to play after all, and suddenly the dimensions of the tie were about to change shape.

Even when Vazquez gratefully accepted Nalbandian's offer to play, he cannot have envisaged the impact Argentina's former leading player would have on the match. The twenty-eight-year-old Nalbandian had played just two matches in nine months after hip surgery in an exhibition event in Buenos Aires and then pulled out with an abductor tear. The injury, however, healed more quickly than he thought, and he had realized he could yet be of

assistance to the Argentine team. So on the eve of the tie he belatedly flew into the Swedish capital.

After a brief look at Nalbandian in practice, Vazquez decided to play him in the doubles alongside Horacio Zeballos, with whom he had never played. It was a risk because Nalbandian could have broken down at any stage, but Vazquez knew what even an 80-percent-fit Nalbandian could give the team.

Unlike most Argentine players, Nalbandian spent his formative years on hard courts in his home city of Cordoba and had won on this same court in Stockholm in 2008 against the Swedish No. 1, Robin Soderling, in the final of the Open. Also that year, he won all three of his rubbers against the Swedes in a Davis Cup quarterfinal in Buenos Aires. If ever there was a man for the job it was Nalbandian. His inclusion, though, did little to alter Thomas Enqvist's resolve that he was about to make a winning start to his career as Sweden's Davis Cup captain, having succeeded Mats Wilander. The opening rubber only reinforced that belief.

Eduardo Schwank, at No. 64 in the world, was ranked nine places higher than Leonardo Mayer, but because the latter was more experienced on hard courts, Schwank was made No. 2 for the Argentine team and had the dubious pleasure of opening against the big-hitting, big-serving Soderling. Not surprisingly, it proved too much for a man playing his first Davis Cup rubber, and he was beaten 6–1 7–6(0) 7–5 by the world No. 7.

Mayer's task was a little easier. Not that Joachim Johansson is a powder-puff puncher compared to Soderling, but the former top 10 player had been out of the game for the best part of sixteen months after a shoulder injury and had only recently returned to top-level tennis.

This was also Mayer's first Davis Cup singles rubber, but he proved that he had learned from his previous experience in a doubles rubber against Czech Republic when nerves, by his own admission, had gotten the better of him. Contrary to what some people may believe, there is more to captaining a Davis Cup team than handing out towels during changeovers, and Vazquez had to find a way of helping Mayer control his emotions. "Basically, it was about getting him to take his time and get his breathing right," explained Vazquez.

Unlike Schwank, the former junior world No. 2 had spent the previous seven months playing solely on hard courts and as a result was much better prepared. Although the first set went against him, he remained faithful to his attacking game and eventually cut the big Swede down to size, winning 5–7 6–3 7–5 6–4 to square the tie.

Enqvist sportingly complimented Mayer on his performance and before the tie even went as far as to say of Nalbandian's inclusion, "We're happy he's here, it's good for everybody—the match, the Swedish crowd—to see such a classic player as Nalbandian."

Pictured below,
clockwise from top left:
Andreas Vinciguerra (SWE);
Leonardo Mayer (ARG);
Robin Soderling (SWE)
Pictured opposite:
David Nalbandian (ARG)

Whether he was still of that opinion three days later was another matter. Aside from the fact that Nalbandian and the left-handed Zeballos had never played together before, the doubles was evenly matched on paper and so it was, too, on court. However, the Argentine pair took an early grip on affairs and never let go, beating Soderling and Robert Lindstedt 6–2 7–6(4) 7–6(5), whereupon Zeballos collapsed into the arms of Nalbandian and then whipped off his shirt and twirled it above his head before doing a victory jig on the team bench. Davis Cup does funny things like that to people.

Nalbandian, playing his first Davis Cup tie since the ill-fated 2008 final against Spain, produced a near-faultless performance. He never dropped serve, returned superbly—as is his wont—and was deft at the net. No wonder he was pleased with himself. "After nine months off the circuit it's not easy to get on court and play well, and I think I did," he said. "My right leg is not 100 percent right so I hope not to be on court for the fifth point tomorrow, but if it's necessary I will."

Unfortunately for Nalbandian it was necessary. Although Mayer put up another spirited performance, it did not stop Soderling from winning his fifth consecutive singles rubber in straight sets, 7–5 7–6(5) 7–5, to square the tie at two-all.

Both captains were then faced with difficult decisions, Enqvist probably more so than Vazquez. Nalbandian had played too well in the doubles to be ignored, but could his leg last the match? Apparently, Argentina only decided to go with him ten minutes

before the tie. As for Enqvist, he was faced with the dilemma of choosing between the fickle force of Johansson and the reliable routineness of Andreas Vinciguerra. He opted for the latter, but Nalbandian's class soon shone through, predictably making irrelevant the 133-place discrepancy in their rankings as he broke the son of an Italian pizza baker to love and secured the first set. Thereafter the world No. 154 upped his game when necessary to win 7–5 6–3 4–6 6–4, leaving the Malmo Redhawks fans wishing the Swedes really had played them at ice hockey rather than tennis. ●

Pictured clockwise
from top left:
David Nalbandian (ARG);
Robert Lindstedt (SWE)
challenges the umpire;
Horacio Zeballos (ARG)

Croatia v Ecuador

It took the magic of Davis Cup to keep Nicolas Lapentti playing, and seventeen years after his first tie in the competition he almost summoned enough strength and craft to topple the giant Ivo Karlovic in the opening rubber of an impossibly difficult first-round match away to Croatia. Sadly, points are not awarded for heroic endeavor, and Ecuador predictably lost 5–0 in the baroque city of Varazdin to a team predicted by many to win the trophy.

The South Americans had already made great strides just to reach this stage of the competition with an away win in the play-offs against Brazil, a result that could not have been more surprising had it been a football match between the two countries. The thirty-three-year-old Lapentti remarked at the time "that it could be the last thing I do," and for many players it would have been an appropriate time to go, given the magnitude of the task that now faced them.

But Lapentti has been nothing if not a fighter throughout his career, as a record number of five-set wins in Davis Cup would testify, and he saw the match in Croatia, playing alongside his brother Giovanni as he has on so many occasions, as just another challenge.

"I'm very happy that I made that decision," he said. "I'm happy to be here, to still be part of tennis. Hopefully, I can compete at a good level and try to go to Croatia and be at the highest level that's possible, to be fit and try to do my best to win that first-round match."

Many would have scoffed at his confidence in succeeding against Karlovic, let alone the world No. 9 Marin Cilic, who had just entered the top 10 for the first time in his career after reaching the semifinals of the Australian Open. It's easy to talk the talk beforehand if one doesn't mind falling flat on one's face later, but backing it up is another matter.

Not that Lapentti was guilty of over-confidence, but he had every reason to be optimistic since he had a winning record against both men due to straight-sets victories over them in two matches in 2008. He had beaten Cilic at the Cincinnati Masters on hard court, a surface almost identical to the one laid at the impressive Varazdin sports complex, while his victory against Karlovic was on carpet in Lyon.

"The Croatians are the favorites to win the tie, especially because Cilic has improved so much in the past year and has surged up the rankings after playing consistently at a very high level," said Lapentti.

"However, Davis Cup is different from the ATP Tour; it's not easy to put the whole team on your shoulders, and Cilic is still a very young player. He needs to be strong mentally, while I am confident that I can beat Karlovic because I know how to play against him. He has a huge serve, and it might come down to a lot of tiebreaks and just a few points."

While Goran Prpic, the Croatia captain, was confident of victory—so confident he had named Antonio Veic and Ivan Dodig to face the Lapentti brothers in the doubles—he was a little concerned about Karlovic playing first against someone as experienced as Nicolas Lapentti. "I would have preferred Cilic to play against Giovanni first, because there is a gulf in class between them, while Nicolas can still play some very good tennis, and if he beats Karlovic, we will be in for a very long weekend," he said. "We are the favorites on paper, but the opening singles rubber may well determine the course of the entire tie."

The big-serving Karlovic sailed through the first set, winning it 6–2, while Lapentti kept his cool, like a boxer soaking up punishment waiting for an opening. It came at the end of the second set and, like the experienced man he is, Lapentti needed just one opportunity to break Karlovic and take the set. It was punch for punch throughout the third set too until the tiebreak when, to the delight of the small clutch of

Ecuadorian fans, Lapentti won six points on the trot to take a two-sets-to-one lead.

It was just as well for Karlovic that his serve was functioning normally—he hit thirty-six aces in the match—because it got him out of trouble time and again. One break in each of the following two sets was enough to give the world No. 29 a 6–2 5–7 6–7(2) 6–3 6–4 victory in three hours and forty-four minutes. Surprisingly, it was only Karlovic's third win in fifteen five-set matches during his career.

"I started well but he came back strongly to win the next two sets, and I was really happy to claw victory from the jaws of defeat after coming from behind," said the exhausted Croat in a courtside interview. "My serve is my most powerful weapon and it didn't let me down, but I knew this was never going to be an easy match."

The second rubber was a much more straightforward affair that Cilic won 6–4 6–3 6–3 against the younger Lapentti in just over two hours. It gave Croatia a 2–0 lead to take into the doubles. Contrary to his original selection, Prpic paid the Lapenttis the respect of playing his first-choice pair against them. Cilic and Karlovic had only played together once before at Queen's two years previously, yet they proved just a little too good for their opponents, winning 7–6(3) 6–3 7–5 to confirm their place in the quarterfinals and a mouth-watering tie at home to neighboring Serbia. ●

White City, Sydney, Australia

The words had barely left Tony Trabert's lips during his loser's speech at Kooyong after the 1953 Davis Cup final when Australia knew it had to start planning for the following year's defense of the title. "I have been playing tennis since I was six years old," said the American No. 1, "but this is the first time I have been beaten by two babies and an old fox."

Trabert was referring to Australia's two precocious nineteen-year-olds, Lew Hoad and Ken Rosewall, and their wily old captain, Harry Hopman, who, along with the doubles player Rex Hartwig, had just pulled off a famous victory against the American team of Trabert and Vic Seixas. A world-record crowd of 17,500 had converged on the old home of the Australian Open in Melbourne, but now it would be moving to Sydney, and interest in what was likely to be another Australia-United States showdown would be huge.

The game, of course, was still amateur in those days, and the New South Wales Lawn Tennis Association, which was charged with organizing the event, knew it would take a full twelve months to bring it about. The White City at Rushcutters Bay Park, one of the largest sports grounds in the world devoted solely to tennis, was chosen as the venue. Its capacity that year had been increased to 10,000, but organizers knew it wouldn't be anywhere near enough to cope with the demand for tickets and temporary stands would have to be erected.

With its imposing two-story colonial clubhouse, from which one could look out over the entire grounds, it was a wonderful center for tennis. When the White City's near forty lawn courts and six hard courts were awash on the weekends with players in their tennis whites, it must have seemed to many an apposite name for the club. In fact, the name came from an amusement park that occupied the site before World War I. When it closed down, the NSWLTA bought it.

In all, seven committees were given various tasks to perform, ranging from organizing media facilities for the two hundred press and radio journalists from around the world who would be covering the tie to supplying the players with needle and cotton "in case of emergencies." One can just imagine Roger and Rafa casting their energy drinks aside today and going for the needle and cotton during changeovers. To darn what, their socks?

The Stands Committee was given the job of, well, building the stands, which cost £50,000 (a vast amount of money in those days). "The scaffolding filled in each of the corners of the White City and towered up to a terrific height—it was an amazing sight," said John Barrett, the former BBC commentator who was a player at the time but attended the tie on his way back from the United States Championships.

Capacity was fixed at what was set to be a world-record figure of 25,188 for a tennis match (later amended to 25,578). In the event, the association received 34,000 ticket applications and £90,000 had to be refunded to disappointed fans. It was a record that stood for fifty years until Spain hosted the 2004 final against the United States before crowds of 27,000 at the Estadio Olimpico de Sevilla (although that was a converted football stadium).

As an indication of the growing interest in the Davis Cup and this then-booming sport, more than 5,000 spectators turned out on Boxing Day just to watch the final practice sessions and then stayed on for the draw. Barrett recalled watching George Worthington, a lesser-known Australian player at the time, giving both Hoad and Rosewall a thorough going over in practice.

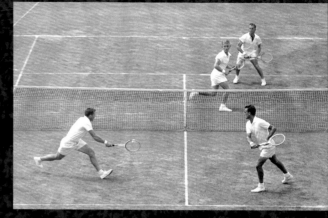

In those days the draw was not dictated by the first name out of the hat, and a cheer went up when Hoad's name immediately followed Trabert's. This meant the tie would open with a rematch between the two players who had produced such an epic encounter in the fourth rubber at Kooyong that to all intents it settled the outcome of that tie, Hoad narrowly winning in five sets.

But the form of the young Australians—the "twins," as they were known—had fallen below expectation in 1954. They had failed to win any of the major singles titles that year. Hoad had missed the Australian Championships due to national service and had also been bothered by a spider bite, while both he and Rosewall had been smitten—by love. Trabert and Seixas, on the other hand, had been fully focused on their tennis all year long, and it showed in the days that followed as three straight wins in the singles and doubles saw the trophy return to the States after four years Down Under.

White City went on to host three more Challenge Round finals, in 1960, 1965, and 1977. The last time it was used for Davis Cup was in 1979, when it staged a semifinal against the States. Until 2000, when the Sydney Olympic Park Tennis Centre was opened, it was the venue of the Medibank International, one of the traditional buildup events to the Australian Open, and was the home of the Australian Tennis Museum from 1983 to 2005. Sadly, its long-term future as a tennis club is unclear after a failed commercial venture at the site led to Administrators being called in. ●

BEHIND THE SCENES

On court, the players are a picture of intensity, focused on one goal of winning the tie. Off court, Davis Cup gives the players a chance to relax in the company of their fellow countrymen, as well as the chance to experience new cultures.

Quarterfinals 9–11 July

Argentina defeated Russia 3–2   MOSCOW, RUSSIA—INDOOR HARD

Czech Republic defeated Chile 4–1   COQUIMBO, CHILE—OUTDOOR CLAY

Serbia defeated Croatia 4–1   SPLIT, CROATIA—INDOOR HARD

France defeated Spain 5–0   CLERMONT-FERRAND, FRANCE—INDOOR HARD

Introduction

If a panel of experts had been asked to forecast the outcome of the quarterfinal round of the 2010 Davis Cup by BNP Paribas when the draw was known, it is unlikely many, if any, would have gotten all four winners correct. In fact, they would have done well to get even a couple right, so surprising were the results. It was classic Davis Cup. More than that, the round produced three emphatic winners.

Who, for instance, could have predicted that France would thrash Spain, the defending champion and arguably the most powerful tennis nation in the world, 5–0? Or that one of the new nations, Serbia, would win 4–1 away against the 2005 champion, Croatia? Russia had not lost on home soil since 1996, so what chance did an Argentine side have without Juan Martin del Potro or Juan Monaco? A very good one, as it turned out, thanks to the irrepressible David Nalbandian.

Russia v Argentina

Russia, unbeaten at home since 1996, against Argentina, without its two highest ranked players. A home win should have been a given, shouldn't it? But there was one unknown factor to bear in mind before jumping to conclusions about the outcome of the quarterfinal in Moscow's Olympic Stadium—and that factor was called David Nalbandian.

Just to make arriving at the final projection a little trickier, whenever Nalbandian is involved there is no point in applying the usual criteria, like form, fitness, or injury. Before he faced the Swedes in the first round, Nalbandian had played just two exhibition matches in nine months after hip surgery and traveled to Stockholm still recovering from injury. The result? He won both his singles rubbers and contributed to the doubles success.

Against the Russians, he hadn't played in nearly three months because of injury, stood at 153 in the rankings (which was at least a couple of hundred places' improvement on what he was in Sweden), and was up against two players ranked 6 and 14 in the world. The outcome? Two wins for Nalbandian in

Similarly, Chile had been beaten just once at home since 1997, and its opponent, Czech Republic, was without the two mainstays of its side—Radek Stepanek and Tomas Berdych. Yet Czech Republic ended up winning 4–1. Of course, there were extenuating circumstances, but it was a good example of the unpredictable nature of the sport (and perhaps one to ward off prospective gamblers).

If some of the favorites were eliminated prematurely from the competition, the semifinal lineup was not only strong, but beautifully balanced. ●

straight sets and Argentina back in the semifinals of Davis Cup after its first win on Russian soil. Of course, it didn't make up for losing the 2006 final in Moscow, but the 3–2 win was gratefully received all the same.

What is it about Nalbandian and the old competition? He seems to save his best form for it. Since losing to the similarly enigmatic Marat Safin— an interested onlooker in Moscow following his retirement—in his first singles rubber in 2002, Nalbandian had won twenty and lost just four after this tie. Tito Vazquez, the Argentine captain, who understands him better than most people, tried to explain: "David is a special guy. He's a guy who has a

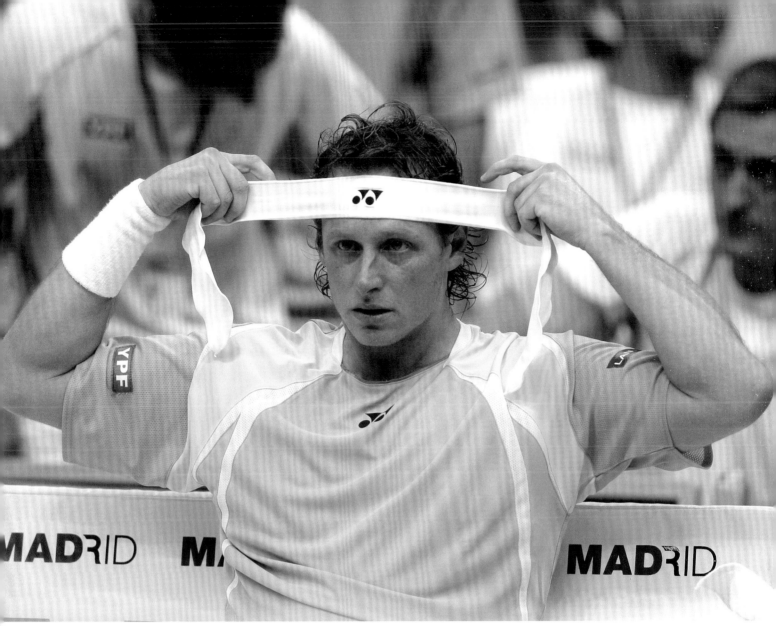

lot of confidence and reads the game very well, and he's a guy who has a lot of variability, which is enough to trouble any player."

Granted, Russian No. 1 Nikolay Davydenko wasn't in the best of shape himself, having missed almost the entire clay-court season because of a wrist injury, but at least he had some matches behind him. Mikhail Youzhny, on the other hand, was in terrific form, having already made three ATP finals and reached the quarterfinals at Roland Garros. But what both players discovered, to their obvious chagrin, was that Nalbandian plays the big points as well, if not better, than anybody, which is something that even the likes of Rafael Nadal and Roger Federer respectfully understand.

Yet Russia went into the tie full of optimism, as any team that has won seventeen ties at home is entitled to do. They also had the wise old Shamil Tarpischev in their corner as usual. It appears

that that in itself is enough for some players, such as Igor Kunitsyn.

"Our captain has done an amazing job throughout the year," said Kunitsyn. "My personal opinion is that he is the best captain in the world right now. He's done it for so many years and he knows what we need to do in every situation: 0–2 down, 2–0 up, losing, winning. He's never nervous and he's always supportive. You feel like he knows all the keys and you just have to follow his orders."

That said, once a player crosses the white line, anything can happen. Davydenko must have known exactly what he had to do to give Russia a winning start on day one, but doing it is something else, particularly when you have a supposed No. 2 like Nalbandian staring you down at the opposite end of the court. Although Nalbandian had a 6–5 advantage in head-to-heads, Davydenko had won during their previous two meetings: Monte Carlo in April, which

Pictured above:
Marat Safin lends his support
alongside Teimuraz Gabashvili (RUS)
on the bench

was the Argentine's last competitive match; and the decisive fourth rubber in Russia's famous 2008 Davis Cup semifinal victory in Buenos Aires, which was the last time Davydenko played Davis Cup.

Even so, this wasn't the same Davydenko who had beaten Argentina's best player, the absent Juan Martin del Potro, to win the Barclays ATP World Tour final in London the previous November, and he sounded as if he was trying to convince himself of his chances when he remarked: "I don't know if he [Nalbandian] will be more confident, as I have played a few matches, some of which went to five sets, while he hasn't really played since the clay-court season."

Nalbandian may have been nearer the mark with his comment: "He's coming back from injury, too, so I think it's going to be tough for both of us."

It was obvious from early on that neither player was at his best, and when that happens a match is generally decided by the one who makes the fewer mistakes. But even that old maxim didn't hold water this time because Nalbandian made sixty-five unforced errors. However, when the points really mattered, the man from Cordoba invariably delivered.

His game plan was much the same as usual: smack anything short. It hadn't escaped his attention that Davydenko was at odds from the baseline, which

meant that his entire game was in peril. Furthermore, his first serve was erratic. "I always believe in my game, and at the beginning I saw he wasn't too solid from the baseline and also with his serve too, so I managed to get things on my side," said Nalbandian. "I tried to play the important points better and we both had a lot of chances today, but I just performed a little better on them."

Davydenko certainly had enough chances, including a double break at the start of the second set, but after two and three-quarter hours he was left scratching his head, a beaten man, 6–4 7–6(5) 7–6(6), and a dejected one, too. "For sure I had a chance in the second set, I had chances in the third set, and I had a set point," he said. "I had many chances but didn't realize them, and I lost. So it's not such a good result for Russia and for me."

Fortunately for Russia, Youzhny hadn't lost a Davis Cup rubber at home in five years and was not about to see his record halted by a player ranked forty-four places beneath him. He easily beat Leonardo Mayer—a second reserve, with Juan Monaco also unavailable because of injury—6–3 6–1 6–4 to level the tie. Youzhny put it down to experience, saying: "He played good, but perhaps he didn't play his best match today. Maybe he hasn't played so

many matches in the Davis Cup, as the Davis Cup is different."

Perhaps because the onus was on the Russians to get a grip on matters, it was they rather than Argentina who opted to gear up their doubles pairing, bringing in Davydenko instead of Teimuraz Gabashvili to partner Kunitsyn, whereas Vazquez chose to rest Nalbandian. The Argentine captain's decision proved a good one, possibly even a decisive one, because Davydenko played just as poorly as he had in the singles, dropping serve five times, and Eduardo Schwank and Horacio Zeballos unexpectedly won 7–6(7) 6–4 6–7(3) 6–1. As is often the case in Davis Cup, the doubles rubber proved decisive.

Neither pair had played together previously in Davis Cup, but the Argentines were confident that the bit of previous history they had of playing together would hold them in good stead. As Zeballos said: "I am really good friends with Schwank, and we were confident, as we are both good doubles players and had played together in the Pan American Games, where we won."

Davydenko was so depressed afterward with his form that he suggested he might not play in the first of the reverse singles the next day against Schwank. As it turned out, his wife had other ideas, as wives often do,

and told him to pull himself together. "I said to my wife, I don't know how I feel, maybe it would be better if I retire today," the Russian said. "She told me, 'You started playing on Friday and you need to continue through till Sunday and win.'"

For one-and-a-half sets it seemed that Davydenko might know more about tennis than his wife, Irina, as he continued to struggle with his game. Then, in the eighth game of the second set, it all started to fall into place, and he finished a convincing 4–6 6–3 6–1 6–4 winner.

And so to the final rubber it went, with Russia still a favorite to win. In fact, Youzhny had a 2–1 lead in head-to-heads against Nalbandian, but both those wins were six years ago, and in their only meeting since, at Monte Carlo this year, the Argentine had won a close three-set match. Just as he had against Davydenko, Nalbandian played the important points better than his opponent and indeed played much better in general than he had two days earlier, enabling him to score another famous Davis Cup victory, 7–6(5) 6–4 6–3.

After such a victory, it was tempting to say "who needs Del Potro?" especially when you have David Nalbandian—the illogical Davis Cup superman—on your side. ●

Chile v Czech Republic

Czech Republic has long claimed it is more than a two-man team, but the absence of Tomas Berdych and Radek Stepanek from the quarterfinal tie in Coquimbo really should have been too much of a handicap for last year's runners-up. In the event, it was absenteeism and fitness issues in the home team's ranks that enabled the Czechs to run out surprisingly easy 4–1 winners.

Fernando Gonzalez is one of the few sportsmen in Chile who can hold his own when it comes to national interest, even when the country's football team is competing at a World Cup, as this one was. So when Gonzo pulled out of the tie three weeks earlier due to injury, interest waned, which was a pity. Not only did a first semifinal since the establishment of the World Group format beckon, but also a first Davis Cup final appearance since 1976, as victory would have given Chile another home tie, against Serbia.

As it was, injury news leading to the event played havoc with both sides' hopes and expectations. Just two days after Gonzalez, who hadn't played in ten weeks, reluctantly withdrew because of a knee injury —"I feel really bad about not playing the competition I like the most," he said—Stepanek, who has had a similarly talismanic effect on his country's Davis Cup fortunes, announced that he, too, was suffering from a knee injury and pulled out. One good luck charm for another; perhaps Chile could yet win this tie.

After all, it had lost just once at home since 1997, and the team's new leader, Nicolas Massu, knew all about Davis Cup, having had fourteen years of experience as a player. Also, he had proved at the 2004 Olympics, when he won gold medals in the singles and doubles, that he was the man for the big occasion. Immediately after the Wimbledon final, the tie took a dramatic swing in Chile's favor when the runner-up, Berdych, announced that due to his incredibly successful and exhausting summer—he also made the semifinals at Roland Garros—he did not feel able to make the long flight to South America.

However, patriotic fervor in Chile was found wanting. The public stayed away in large numbers,

Pictured below:
Jorge Aguilar (CHI) and Nicolas Massu (CHI);
The Chilean fans

Pictured above:

Lukas Dlouhy (CZE) and Jan Hajek (CZE)

unexpected reverse. There was a discrepancy of 146 places in the players' rankings—only it was Massu who should have been emphasizing the difference in class.

Minar, who had only played two previous singles rubbers and had lost them both, maintained his grip on the match throughout, and with the Chilean contributing greatly to his own downfall with an unacceptable number of unforced errors, the Czech won 6–0 6–2 6–3. It was only natural that Minar should equate the result to the Challenger background from which he comes, saying: "Now that Davis Cup has points for the world rankings, this is like having won a Challenger."

It was a chastening experience for Massu but not one that surprised him too much. "I am not very fit these days," he said with a disarming frankness. "I have just played two tournaments in the last two months. I came here knowing I was not very well. I always felt the ball coming to me quicker than what I wanted it to, and I felt that I did not have enough strength to hit it."

Although the loss of Berdych and Stepanek was obviously a huge blow to Jaroslav Navratil's team, it was to Czech Republic's good fortune that both the players who stepped in for them were clay-court specialists. In fact, one could argue they were even more at home on the surface than either of the first-choice players. Jan Hajek, who represented them in the second rubber, had beaten Stepanek in the final of the Prostejov Challenger just a month earlier.

At Wimbledon, he had gone out in the first round to Great Britain's Andy Murray, but here on the red stuff at the Enjoy Tennis Center in Coquimbo he was much more at home. There wasn't much to enjoy for the home patrons on day one, though, as he thrashed Paul Capdeville 6–0 6–2 6–1 to put the Czech team firmly in command. It was one of the worst opening days in Chile's illustrious history—winning just eight games in six sets is an appalling return. Hans Gildemeister, Chile's captain, had put his faith in Capdeville rather than Jorge Aguilar, but it had not been rewarded. It was the Chilean's fifth defeat in his last six singles rubbers.

Hajek, on the other hand, was ecstatic. The Czechs had requested that their press conferences be conducted in their native language because their English wasn't good. Their physiotherapist, who had lived in Spain, translated, and through him Hajek said: "Radek [Stepanek] and Tomas [Berdych] are our best

partly due to the ticket prices (the cheapest was about $40), and partly due to other financial commitments, such as winter vacations and new LCD televisions bought in anticipation of watching Chile win the World Cup. Had they known that Massu was nursing a back injury they would have been even less enthusiastic.

The new Chilean No. 1 was set to face Ivo Minar, a clay-court player but not one of his caliber, in the opening rubber. Massu had only ever lost two singles rubbers at home, both in 2007, and it took the Russians Marat Safin and Igor Andreev to inflict them. A quick win would lift Chilean spirits, it was thought, and make the public realize that this was not an event to be missed. Sadly for the home team, it didn't quite work out like that. Before Massu's back had had a chance to loosen up, Minar had taken the first set 6–0 in thirty-one minutes. Suddenly Chile was staring at an

players, but we have shown that we can be there if they are not able to be in future ties."

Indeed they had. What the absence of the top men also meant was that for once, Lukas Dlouhy, who almost any country in the world would love to have in its team, was an almost certain starter in the doubles. Dlouhy is a two-time Grand Slam doubles champion but rarely gets the chance to play in his preferred event in Davis Cup due to the omnipotence of Berdych and Stepanek. He was scheduled to play alongside another doubles specialist, Frantisek Cermak, but in the event it was Hajek who partnered him, and the rookie pair secured victory by beating Aguilar and Massu 7–6(3) 6–3 3–6 6–3.

If nothing else, Chile had finally won a set when they took advantage of Dlouhy's frailty on serve, a possible hangover from Wimbledon, where he committed an uncharacteristic number of double faults and went out of the competition prematurely. Massu, who was again well below par, did his best to remain upbeat. "I cannot forget that we are among the best eight countries in the world," he said. "We have been there, among the best first ten or fifteen nations in the world, for the last six or seven years. Not many countries can say so, and our country is small, yet we have done a lot. It's a shame not everybody understands that."

Of course, he was absolutely right. As for Chile's future, that looks bleak: none of the current youngsters have come anywhere near equaling the junior achievements of Gonzalez and Massu, never mind Marcelo Rios. A period outside the World Group seems inevitable. Victory in one dead rubber, when Aguilar beat Dlouhy, was no compensation for a country of their reputation.

As for Czech Republic, it proved that it has strength in depth—but then we always knew that. ●

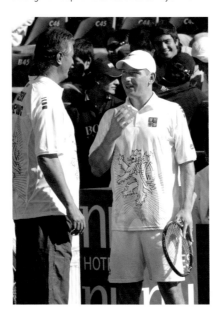

Pictured above:
Ivo Minar (CZE);
Relief for the Czechs
Pictured below:
Jan Hajek (CZE) with captain Jaroslav Navratil

Croatia v Serbia

Tennis, like so much in life, is all about timing. Had Croatia's historic meeting with Serbia in Split come in spring rather than summer there might have been a completely different outcome to this quarterfinal. Ivo Karlovic and Mario Ancic were both fit then, while Ivan Ljubicic, who came out of Davis Cup retirement to replace the former, was playing the best tennis of his life, having just won the BNP Paribas Open in Indian Wells.

Throw in the additional and not inconsiderable advantage of a fiercely partisan Croatian crowd and it might all have been a bit too much for a Serbian team that was not renowned for its ability to travel. But as the old sports cliché would have it, you can only beat what's placed in front of you, and Novak Djokovic and company did that remarkably well to reach the first semifinal in their country's short history. Besides, Croatia won the title in 2005. It was about time its

talented former countrymen had the chance to show the world what they're made of.

They had beaten the multiple champions, United States, to get this far, and Djokovic, who had risen to No. 2 in the world, Nenad Zimonjic, who was joint No. 1 in doubles, and the versatile Janko Tipsarevic were in no mood to pull up short now. Along with Viktor Troicki they have built up a good team spirit, which was to stand them in good stead in what they knew would be a very difficult tie mentally, if not physically.

As usual, Djokovic had his parents present to provide moral support, but, more surprisingly, he also had his younger brother, eighteen-year-old Marko,

along as first reserve, which drew criticism from some quarters of the Serbian media, which felt there were other players more deserving of the experience than the No. 1300–ranked Djokovic.

The pressure of expectation, however, was all on Croatia, and Goran Prpic, the captain and former Yugoslav Davis Cup player, clearly felt it. "It's a pity that in these conditions we play at home in Split and they all expect us to win."

They may have been all one country not so long ago, but there is no such thing as divided loyalties when it comes to sporting contests between these two young nations—the only exception, perhaps, being the former Yugoslav player Niki Pilic, who captained Croatia when it won the title but has been an advisor to the Serbian team for the past three years. Wisely, he decided to stay at home.

History was around every corner of this tie, starting with the draw, which was held at Villa Dalmajica, the summer residence of the former Yugoslav president Josip Broz Tito. The magnificent villa was built on Marjan Hill, a dormant volcano on the Split Peninsula, close to the shores of the beautiful Dalmatian coast. When Karlovic failed a late fitness test on his Achilles injury that morning, the Croatian team looked for all the world like a dormant volcano, too. Djokovic had a winning record against both Marin Cilic and Ljubicic, whom he faced first, but not the giant Karlovic, who had beaten him in both their hard-court encounters.

"Karlovic is a tricky opponent on any surface for anybody because of his serve—he is one of the best servers who ever played the game," conceded Djokovic, "but, still, Ljubicic is back, which brings a lot of joy to the Croatian team."

And to the Serbian team, one could safely bet. Since winning his tenth career title in the Masters-1000 event at Indian Wells at the ripe old age of thirty-one, Ljubicic had been plagued by injuries, most of which he was now over, but he was short of match practice. He had been retired from Davis Cup for three-and-a-half years but had promised Prpic that if he needed him in an emergency he would be there. That emergency had arrived.

His only hope would be that Djokovic had failed to recover completely from his run to the Wimbledon

semifinals just a week earlier and would struggle with the change of surface from grass to indoor court, which the Serbian described as "the cruelty of the sport." As it happened, Djokovic managed the physical side of things effortlessly and the transition seamlessly.

Unfortunately for the Serbian team, their fans were conspicuously absent at the Spaladium Arena, but on reflection it was probably just as well. The treatment the Serbian national anthem received on the opening day was so disrespectful that even Ljubicic found it off-putting. "You could feel the tension; you could feel the emotion, so it was really difficult for me to play the first couple of games," he said.

It wasn't exactly easy for Djokovic either, and the 4–1 lead the Serb was gifted early on soon vanished under a welter of crowd noise that even an experienced umpire like Carlos Ramos could do little to alleviate. It's situations like this that make or break players in Davis Cup, and Djokovic, to his credit, pulled through like an old trouper. The fearsome Ljubicic serve had managed to take the first set to a tiebreak, which he lost, but it was the loss of the second set, in which he had real chances, that hurt him more. After that there was only one possible outcome: a 7–6(3) 6–4 6–1 win for the former Australian Open champion.

"It's sensitive circumstances that we play in, considering the situation between the two countries that they had twenty years back, and, of course, it's still very fresh [in the mind]," said Djokovic, adding diplomatically: "We are professional athletes and tennis players and we don't involve politics in sport. We want to perform our best for the country and win; that's what I did today and in the end I got a nice appreciation from the crowd for what I have done today so this is what I remember from the match."

Cilic was favored to level the tie against Troicki, even though he had been unable to sustain that stunning form of the early season when he reached the semifinals of the Australian Open. There was a wobble when he found himself trailing 5–2 with set point against him in the second, but other than that it was a fairly straightforward 6–4 7–5 6–2 victory and his fifth in succession against his opponent. Bogdan Obradovic, the Serbian captain, thought he saw signs of pressure building up in Cilic (but then, he would).

A doubles rubber against Zimonjic and Tipsarevic called for desperate measures from the Croatian captain, and he decided that the abilities of Cilic would have to be utilized to the maximum, selecting him to play alongside Ivan Dodig, but it was all to no avail. The Serbian pair was far too good for a rookie pair and won easily 6–3 6–2 6–4 to restore its country's lead. Croatia's only hope now was that Cilic would surprise Djokovic, because in that event the experienced Ljubicic would be the likely favourite to beat Troicki in a decisive final rubber. As it turned out, Cilic was nowhere near good enough.

It takes a lot to silence a crowd from Split, but Djokovic managed it superbly with some powerful, aggressive tennis to win his high-noon showdown with Cilic 6–3 6–3 6–2 in just two hours, twenty-four minutes. His opponent was too passive at the start, taking just seven points from the first five games, but when he tried to slug it out with his young rival he was invariably worse off. It wasn't difficult to see why Cilic had now won just one set in five matches against the Serb. It was only when Djokovic struck the winning shot that he hinted he was human after all, collapsing flat on his back. But he was up on his feet exchanging high-fives with his ecstatic teammates when the Croatian crowd sportingly chose to applaud them with their cheerstix.

"Personally, I had a lot of responsibility with the package that I carried on my back before this tie, but right now I feel so relieved that we won," said Djokovic. "We won in one of the toughest atmospheres against a team that has had a lot of success in this competition."

Afterward Cilic tipped them to go all the way. "They have a good team—a really good team, actually," he said. "With their own crowd I think they can go to the final." ●

Pictured above:

The Croatian fans;

Nenad Zimonjic (SRB) and Janko Tipsarevic (SRB)

Pictured opposite:

Novak Djokovic (SRB) celebrates;

Ivan Ljubicic (CRO)

www.daviscup.com

France v Spain

It's hard enough in the best of times to envisage Spain losing a Davis Cup tie, but 5–0? Suffice to say that it is no less surprising than if their newly crowned world champion football team lost 5–0. While it would have been interesting to see what would have happened had Rafael Nadal been present, it would be churlish to use his absence as an excuse, and Albert Costa, the defending champion's captain, did not attempt to do so.

France, whose own leading man, Jo-Wilfried Tsonga, was out because of a knee injury, was a thoroughly deserving winner of this extraordinary quarterfinal at Clermont-Ferrand—the headquarters of Michelin—which in tennis terms was at least the equivalent of a three-star award from the famous restaurant guide. It was certainly a feast of tennis for those fortunate to have been present over the course of the three days at the Zenith-Grande Halle d'Auvergne.

It's normal in sport to try to shift the burden of favoritism onto the opposition, but Guy Forget, the France captain, was hardly stretching a point when he described Spain as favorites on the eve of the tie. "Spain is favorite on paper and they are playing better than we are, but we have nothing to lose," he said. "We have great potential with four players playing well. We miss Jo [Tsonga] and Richard [Gasquet], but

we have a lot of depth in French tennis and hopefully that will be enough."

Since winning Davis Cup for the first time in 2000, Spain has won it on four more occasions, including last year's 5–0 final against Czech Republic. It can also boast no fewer than seven players in the world's top 25. In fact, Nadal was the only top player who was unavailable, and he was most reluctant to pull out of what he described as "a special confrontation." He had decided instead to undergo new treatment that he hoped would cure his knee problems once and for all and enable him to arrive at the US Open in better shape than he usually does.

In his place, Fernando Verdasco, the world No. 10, stepped in—not a bad replacement. It's not unusual for Davis Cup to play a crucial part in a player's career, but it is rarely so obviously career changing as it was for the madrileño in 2008, and he acknowledges that fact. His career was jogging along quite nicely when he was selected to play in the final against Argentina that year, but when he ended up winning the fifth and final rubber against Jose Acasuso, the manner in which he handled the enormous pressure had a profound effect upon him.

"Just one month later I did the semis in Australia and I went into the top ten for the first time in my life," he recalled. "The confidence, the spirit, everything that

the tie in Argentina gave me, like a person, like a player, it was so much, so important for me. After that everything changed so much."

For Gael Monfils, once the French Open is behind him in a season, the Davis Cup becomes his priority, and he spoke quite charmingly beforehand about the prospect of France winning and having "a really nice story to talk about later." It was a story that had not been recounted in eighty-seven years—that was the last time, the only time, France, the nine-time champion, had beaten Spain, which put the size of its challenge into perspective. But, a little surprisingly, in six meetings the teams had never played on an indoor hard court, and this one was going to be fast, very fast, laid in a horseshoe-shaped arena (for good luck?).

Feliciano Lopez is a player who likes fast courts—he had beaten Nadal at Queen's a couple of months earlier—and there was speculation that Verdasco might be held back for the reverse singles since he had some foot issues and had turned his ankle in training. As it transpired, he was named for the maximum three rubbers, as was France's Michael Llodra, while Monfils was drawn to open against David Ferrer. At the pre-match dinner, even Forget was rooting for Spain—in its World Cup semifinal against Germany, which was considerably shown on large screens for the benefit of the guests. Would the 1–0 victory for Spain be an inspiration for its tennis counterparts? We were about to find out.

Understandably, Monfils, who surprisingly only made his Davis Cup debut the previous September, was a little nervous at the start, but having beaten Ferrer in their only meeting, albeit on clay in the quarterfinals of the 2008 French Open, he knew he had nothing to fear. He took the first set on a tiebreak and with some penetrating deep returns sailed through the second set. However, there is no more dogged player in the game today than the Spaniard, and unsurprisingly he came back into it to square the match.

Pictured above:
David Ferrer (ESP) and captain Albert Costa
Pictured below:
The Zenith-Grande Halle d'Auvergne

In the final set Monfils went 3–0 ahead, then 4–1, and then served for the match at 5–4, only for Ferrer to claw his way back. But with Forget telling him to "be like a boxer and keep fighting," Monfils stayed on his toes and jabbed his way to a 7–6(3) 6–2 4–6 5–7 6–4 victory.

The French crowd's excitement was stifled somewhat when Verdasco won the first set against Llodra on a tiebreak. But with the Spaniard struggling with his serve (and as a result his composure), the thirty-year-old Llodra took advantage and calmly set about playing "almost the best tennis I have ever played" to score a famous 6–7(5) 6–4 6–3 7–6(2) victory. "I told my team that, on a fast court like this one, if they were really aggressive and going for their shots, we had a chance," said Forget. "Our best chance was actually to go forward and not to wait for the Spanish to miss because they hardly miss."

Suddenly history was overwhelmingly on France's side. Some statistical wizard had worked out that in the 105 matches that France had taken a 2–0 lead, it had gone on to win 103 times. To add to the statistics in France's favor, Spain had never come back from 0–2 down. Nevertheless, as we all know, it's never over until the fat lady opens her lungs, and the Marseillaise, which was sung at the start of the second day's play, had to wait its turn for a reprise.

Llodra and Julien Benneteau—two singles specialists—have been building up a fine rapport,

which has been playing a major part in the team's success. It has obviously helped that they are continuing their partnership outside of Davis Cup: they reached the quarterfinals at Wimbledon and won the Open 13 tournament at Marseille. Here they were the more cohesive unit. They went on the attack from the start and only briefly let the initiative slip, beating Lopez and Verdasco 6–1 6–2 6–7(6) 7–6(5) to put the nine-time champion into the last four for the first time in six years.

"Today it was too good on the court," said Llodra. "When I started playing tennis, my dream was to play in the French team. When I was eleven years old, I saw Guy Forget and Henri Leconte in Davis Cup in Lyon when they won against the USA and, in my head, you know I said one time in my life I want to be like this and today it was amazing. We beat Spain, the defending champions. It's unbelievable."

It was Spain's first defeat since losing to the United States, the eventual champions, in the 2007 quarterfinals. But worse was to come for them when, on an irrelevant third day, Gilles Simon beat Nicolas Almagro 7–6(4) 7–6(7) and Benneteau beat Lopez 7–6(3) 6–4. It was only the second time since the formation of the World Group in 1981 that the defending champion had lost a tie 5–0; in the 2003 quarterfinals Russia lost 5–0 to Argentina. So there was a nice symmetry to France's semifinal meeting with the Argentines.

"It's been a few years since we've been in the semifinals," said Forget, "but we have a young group of players who have improved every year and I think now is their time." ●

Squeezed in the corner of the grounds of the Club Atletico River Plate, this temporary stadium looked more like an apology than a proud statement of how far Argentine tennis had come. Built largely of scaffolding and wood, it was endearingly christened Monumentalito after the famous football stadium that towered above it and yet, in 2003, it became the scene of an extraordinary triumph for the host nation; in fact two monumental ones.

The visit of the Davis Cup champion, Russia, in April of that year demanded a venue with greater capacity than the charming, old-world Buenos Aires Lawn Tennis Club—the regular venue for Davis Cup ties in the capital—could manage. The company hired to stage the federation's home ties had already built a temporary arena in the grounds of the River Plate football club for the first-round tie against Germany two months earlier, so it made sense to utilize the facility once more before demolishing it. Apart from anything else, it held good memories for Gustavo Luza's players, who had beaten the Germans 5–0.

Whoever erected it must have known nothing about the mental fragility of tennis players. Either that or they decided that Argentina's were now oblivious to

noise after several years of wildly enthusiastic home support. Just a few meters behind the stand at one end of the court thundered eight lanes of motorway traffic, while down the middle of the highway ran a railway line (considerate train drivers would honk their horns as they rattled by when the tennis was on).

In addition, planes roared overhead on their way in and out of nearby Jorge Newberry Airport. One assumes that reports of them being within touching distance of spectators in the upper rows of the temporary stands were a slight exaggeration. It made Flushing Meadows seem like a library.

"It is a little strange to hear trains and planes while tennis is going on," commented Verena von Schonfeldt of German television. "I suppose it's a reflection of what Buenos Aires is like as a city—lots of noise."

More than thirty thousand tickets were sold for the three days' play, which beat by a couple of thousand the record set when Argentina played United States twenty years earlier. While there were numerous complaints from fans about the facilities provided—like the lack of proper access in and out of the stadium and the fact there were only five toilets for ten thousand people—none was about the standard of tennis put on by their team.

Argentina was a rising force at that time: David Nalbandian, the No. 1, had just reached his first (and only) Grand Slam final, at Wimbledon, while Gaston Gaudio was nearing the peak of his powers. The latter's victory in the dead rubbers on the final day was his thirteenth consecutive one at home, an Argentine record.

Against that, Shamil Tarpischev's team was without the services of its No. 1 player, Marat Safin, who had steered Russia to a dramatic first title success against France in Paris just four months earlier. He had aggravated an ankle injury in practice and was forced to pull out, while Mikhail Youzhny, the young hero of Paris, looked completely out of sorts. Safin became the object of much teasing by the Argentine fans, particularly the River Plate ones who were attending a football match at the Monumental stadium on the Sunday, but having spent his formative years in Barcelona, he was able to give as good as he got.

"They shouted out to him that he was afraid to play, but typical of Marat he took it well and came back with some comments of his own. It was all good fun, and he soon became more of an idol than an enemy to them," said the Spanish umpire, Enric Molina.

The weather on the opening day was all over the place, and the first rubber, between Nalbandian and Davydenko, was interrupted three times by rain. The Russian was not the player he is today but a modest No. 64 in the rankings, and he was soundly beaten in straight sets by the bullish young man from Cordoba. The more experienced but aging Yevgeny Kafelnikov suffered a similar fate at the hands of Gaudio. The Russian was not the only one put to flight: someone counted eight planes flying overhead during just one of Gaudio's service games.

However, Kafelnikov was positive afterward about both his game and the hosts' hospitality. "The crowd was excellent, too," he said. "I expected empty Coke cans thrown on the court at me, but they were pretty well behaved."

Only empty ones? The Russians made a slightly better fist of it in the doubles, but Kafelnikov and Youzhny were still no match for Lucas Arnold and Nalbandian, losing to them in four sets. The Argentines had just beaten the champions, but they celebrated as if they had won the Davis Cup itself, dancing across the wooden floorboards while the Russians trudged off to the locker rooms—or should I say the Portakabins? ●

HIGHS AND LOWS

Tennis players are used to the thrill of a win or the frustration of a loss, but in Davis Cup these emotions are intensified because they are not competing for themselves—they are representing their country.

Semifinals 17–19 September

France defeated Argentina 5–0 LYON, FRANCE—INDOOR HARD

Serbia defeated Czech Republic 3–2 BELGRADE, SERBIA—INDOOR HARD

Introduction

The Davis Cup by BNP Paribas got the final that most neutral observers—and not a few partial ones—wanted: Serbia versus France. First-time finalists at home versus nine-time winners. It couldn't have been better balanced.

But each team's respective route to the Belgrade final could not have been more contrasting: Serbia had to fight tooth and claw to scramble its way past USA (3–2), Croatia away (4–1), and Czech Republic (3–2), while France negotiated a hazardous route with ridiculous ease in disposing of Germany (4–1), Spain (5–0), and Argentina (5–0).

Perhaps fate was acting as a fifth man for the Serbian team—although if it was it has a mischievous way of realizing a country's destiny. When Novak Djokovic, Serbia's leading man and undoubted inspiration, withdrew from the singles on the morning of the first day of the semifinal against the Czech Republic with a stomach complaint, it seemed that Serbia's dream of playing in a first final had been cruelly dashed.

By unexpectedly finishing the first day's singles all square, however, Serbia had high hopes prior to the doubles, in which a point has been a virtual banker ever since Nenad Zimonjic played and won his first Davis Cup doubles match six years ago. But to the whole of Serbia's disbelief, he and Djokovic—back from his illness—lost to Radek Stepanek and Tomas Berdych. Again a nation was plunged into despair.

Coming from 2–1 down to win against a team as good as the Czechs seemed a mighty big ask. Djokovic's quality is a given, but so, too, is Janko Tipsarevic's appetite for the big occasion (remember the 2008 Australian Open and the scare he gave the then-invincible Roger Federer?). And let's not forget the 2010 US Open in which he beat home favorite Andy Roddick.

France would have to be wary of his mental strength and Djokovic's qualities, of course, but after an outstanding year, it was not going to start doubting itself for one moment. Anyone who thought France's 5–0 win against Spain in the quarterfinals was a fluke was made to think again by the manner in which the team severely dealt with David Nalbandian et al.

The French may not possess a player of Djokovic's star quality but it has an enviable strength in depth and a self-belief that gets stronger with every tie. Other countries can be grateful that Davis Cup teams number just four players instead of twice that many; otherwise France really would be unbeatable!

Guy Forget's new millennium musketeers are certain to do their country proud in the years to come, but for now all eyes were on the intriguing final in the hothouse of the Belgrade Arena. ●

France v Argentina

As hard acts to follow go, beating Spain 5–0 is about as daunting as it gets. So it was just as well for France that the semifinal against Argentina in Lyon was more about the result than the performance. As it turned out, Guy Forget's team delivered in both respects as France brought an eight-year hiatus to an end by reaching the Davis Cup final and again forced its celebrated opposition to suffer a whitewash.

France's captain had told his players beforehand that they must be "ready to die on the court." Fortunately, it didn't come to that, because France was unquestionably the stronger team throughout the weekend. For once this year in Davis Cup, the Nalbandian factor played no part in the outcome of

a tie, which was strange because the Argentine was in better shape physically than he had been in his two previous ties after an active and successful summer.

Had Juan Martin del Potro, Argentina's No. 1 player, been fit in time, things might have been different. Then again, France was without arguably its best player, Jo-Wilfried Tsonga, while injury also denied Julien Benneteau, who had been outstanding against Spain, a place on the team.

France's strength in depth, of course, has been obvious for many years, but recently its younger players seem to have matured. They no longer appear to be intimidated by the pressure of Davis Cup. One senses that if it came down to a fifth rubber—as it did the last time France was in a Davis Cup final, in 2002—it would be unlikely for any French player to lose from two sets to love up, like the unfortunate Paul-Henri Mathieu famously did against Russia's Mikhail Youzhny.

Having so many good players to choose from has meant that France hasn't had to blood the younger ones in Davis Cup before they were ready. It's amazing to think that Gael Monfils, who seems to have been around for years, hadn't played Davis Cup before September 2009. Ahead of the semifinals, the twenty-four-year-old had won both his singles rubbers, which had kicked off victories against Germany and Spain. Here, he played in the second, all-important rubber against Nalbandian—not a matchup for the fainthearted.

However, it may have surprised some people to learn that he had won both their previous meetings, on hard courts, in straight sets, two years earlier. But this is Davis Cup, a competition in which Nalbandian thrives (he is desperate to win before he retires). Also, he came into this one in good form, having won the Legg Mason Tennis Classic in Washington in August and immediately afterward reached the quarterfinals of the Toronto Cup, where he beat world No. 4 Robin Soderling. "I didn't start the year well, but there was the hope to play Davis Cup always because I really like it," he said.

His performances in the competition during the year had been nothing short of heroic when, despite inactivity due to hip surgery and a hamstring injury, he had managed to win the decisive final rubbers against both Sweden and Russia. But he was cautious about this tie. "It's going to be tough," he said. "I think it's going to be tougher than Russia."

Monfils was in no mean form himself, having reached the quarterfinals at the US Open, which was as far as he had ever traveled in a Grand Slam on hard courts. Forget, of course, did not underestimate the size of the task facing his young player: "David is one of the best players in the world indoors, and on a good day he can beat the best players in the world," he said—but he also knew that Monfils could be swept to victory by the crowd at the Palais des Sport, just as Forget himself had been nineteen years earlier when it carried him to victory against Pete Sampras to give Yannick Noah's France the title.

Being French, Monfils is not afraid to admit he can be emotional, but he sees it as a strength rather than a weakness. "For an emotional player like me to play in Davis Cup is just something unbelievable," he said. "You're not playing for yourself, you're playing for your flag. You have your whole country behind you, an unbelievable crowd, your friends on the side, your captain on the chair. There's a different spirit."

It was with these thoughts uppermost in his mind that he went into battle against Nalbandian. He broke the Argentine in the opening game and then opened up a 4–1 lead. Nalbandian got back one of the breaks but it was not enough. Although he won the second set, the 6–2 margin was misleading, because every game was hard-fought.

One break in the third game of the third set by Monfils was enough to clinch it. Nalbandian used to be famous for his five-set wars of attrition, and when he opened up a 3–0 lead in the fourth set it looked as though he could be dragging the more athletic Monfils into another of those brutal toe-to-toe slugfests. It was then that the crowd intervened, lifting the Frenchman in a quite extraordinary way as he went on to win the next six games, securing the match 6–4 2–6 6–4 6–3.

"I knew before it would be an amazing experience and it is, it is," said a both excitable and emotional Monfils afterward. "I would like to say thanks to the French crowd, they have been behind me during all the match. It's like they gave me wings so I was flying on the court. You can't reach every ball, but this helped me a lot."

France was flying, too, because it was now 2–0 up. After coming from behind to beat a world No. 10 player in Fernando Verdasco in Clermont-Ferrand in the quarterfinals, Michael Llodra was expected to beat Juan Monaco, making his return to Davis Cup after a wrist injury. It was far from being a formality, because the Argentine held a 2–1 lead in head-to-head meetings, all on hard courts, but again Llodra rose to the challenge, and after a nervous start his serve began working sweetly and he ran out a reasonably comfortable 7–5 4–6 7–5 6–3 winner.

"I've seen it all in Davis Cup throughout the years: you don't expect anything because anything can happen," Forget said later. "All the matches are always crucial and all the guys always give their best in this competition, more than any other tournament."

Because of the injury to Benneteau, Forget had to look for a new partner for Llodra in the doubles and inevitably opted for the thirty-two-year-old Arnaud Clement, who used to regularly partner him in Davis

Cup, in the hope that they could revive that old "magic." In fact, the last time the two played together in Davis Cup they scored a famous victory over USA's Bryan brothers, but that was two-and-a-half years ago. Also, Forget had to bear in mind that the thirty-year-old Llodra would be playing on successive days and had rolled his ankle in the singles.

The Argentines, Horacio Zeballos and Eduardo Schwank, only came together in July in the quarterfinal against Russia, scoring a crucial victory over Nikolay Davydenko and Igor Kunitsyn. It had encouraged them—in preparation for this tie—to get together at the US Open, where they surprised many people by reaching the semifinals. So it was a nicely poised rubber in prospect and had the added spice of possibly determining who went through to the final.

As it transpired, it was surprisingly one-sided. The Zeballos serve was placed under pressure throughout the opening set and was broken twice, in the sixth and tenth games. Early in the second set it was Schwank's turn to be broken, at which point Llodra leaped into the air in celebration. No worries about the ankle now. Although the Argentines broke straight back, everyone knew Llodra wasn't jumping to conclusions.

Zeballos and Schwank stayed with their opponents—who are both Wimbledon doubles champions—until the twelfth game, when, on France's third break point, Clement hit a backhand cross-court winner to take the set. The quality of Llodra's service was only matched by that of his service returns, while Clement gave first-class support. The game—and the tie—was up for the Argentines when Schwank dropped serve in the sixth game of the third set and soon after the Frenchmen completed a 6–4 7–5 6–3 victory.

"It was like we played [together] yesterday," remarked a deliriously happy Clement. "It is very easy to find Michael on the court."

And so France became only the fourth nation since the advent of the World Group in 1981 to reach the final without losing a live rubber. No country has gone all the way without doing so. "I am so proud to lead a team like this one," said Forget. "They have gone through a lot of things together.... They struggled a bit last year, but to see them on the court celebrating emotionally is very strong."

As for Argentina, which has twice reached the final in the last four years, it remains the best country never to have won the Davis Cup, a sobriquet probably about as unwanted as that which attached itself to Nalbandian a few years ago: "the best player never to have won a Grand Slam." Nevertheless, Tito Vasquez, the captain, was rightly proud of his young team members, who, without Del Potro, had gone further in the competition than anyone—probably including themselves—had expected.

All that was left for the French team to do was to turn their attention to Belgrade, where Czech Republic had taken a surprise 2–1 lead against Serbia, and pray that Radek Stepanek and company could squeeze out one more victory in the reverse singles. It didn't happen. A win for the Czechs meant France would have been at home in the final, held tight to the nation's bosom, with the chance to avenge last year's defeat against those opponents. But the win for Serbia would now see them thrown into the cauldron that is the Belgrade Arena.

Forget made no attempt to minimize how onerous a task that would be, describing it as "a nightmare for the players" but adding that they were no longer innocents abroad. If they managed to pull off a tenth Davis Cup triumph there, he felt, it would be comparable to the famously unexpected victory he led them to in Australia in 2001. ●

Pictured below:

The Palais des Sports de Gerland;
Juan Monaco (ARG), David Nalbandian (ARG)
and Eduardo Schwank (ARG)

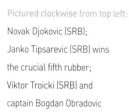

Pictured clockwise from top left:
Novak Djokovic (SRB);
Janko Tipsarevic (SRB) wins
the crucial fifth rubber;
Viktor Troicki (SRB) and
captain Bogdan Obradovic

Serbia v Czech Republic

There were more twists and turns to the Serbia versus Czech Republic semifinal than on the street circuit of Monaco, where three of the star players in this tie reside. At the start it was clear that if Serbia was to keep its appointment with destiny—its first appearance in a Davis Cup final—it would have to endure a fairly tortuous journey in order to do so.

Some things never change. The last time the old country of Yugoslavia stood on the brink of such a historic achievement, in 1991, the Croatian War of Independence broke out, and the two Gorans, Ivanisevic and Prpic, being Croatian, were obliged to withdraw their services. A patched-up Yugoslav team ended up losing 5–0 in the final to France.

The same opposition lay in wait for them this time, too, providing Serbia could beat last year's runners-up and France could deal with Argentina. Now, as before, its team was massively disrupted, although on this occasion, thankfully, because of injury rather than civil war.

Just three hours before an expectant crowd of 17,000 welcomed their heroes on court on day one at the Belgrade Arena, Serbia's talisman, Novak Djokovic—the man who had pushed Rafael Nadal to his considerable limits just four days earlier in the US Open final—withdrew from the opening rubber, complaining of "acute gastroenteritis." The entire Serbian nation was left clutching its stomach, too, after such a blow. This was not how things were supposed to go on the biggest day of its federation's short life.

Djokovic seemed to be the only man in the arena who wasn't concerned, saying he had complete faith in his replacement, Viktor Troicki. As he pointed out in a television interview, Troicki was an accomplished player, as he had proven by just recently taking Djokovic himself to five sets in the first round of the US Open.

In fact, Troicki was only a few points away from denying Djokovic his joyous homecoming prior to this tie. But the 2008 Australian Open champion is the one on whom the country places most of its hopes and so

Pictured opposite:

Janko Tipsarevic (SRB) and
the victorious Serbian team

Pictured above:

Tomas Berdych (CZE);
Serbian fans

far he had not let them down, winning his four singles rubbers during the year. His performance in the intimidating atmosphere of Split's Spaladium Arena against Croatia in the previous round was particularly bold and brave.

Now he could only look on helplessly while Troicki tried in vain to dominate the artful Radek Stepanek. Meanwhile, the crowd was left fretting over whether Djokovic would play any part in this tie and, if he did, in what sort of physical condition he would be. Little did they know that a less celebrated member of the Serbian team would come to the rescue, thereby underlining this young country's strength in depth.

As Troicki's big serve carried him through the first set, hopes were high that he would find a way to defeat his opponent in straight sets, just as he had done on two occasions the month before. At that time, however, Stepanek was still struggling to recover from mononucleosis, which can be particularly tough when you are pushing thirty-two, as well as some injuries. But then this was Davis Cup, in which he always seems able to pull out that little bit extra. And this tie proved no exception.

It didn't take Stepanek long to work out that drop shots and lobs were the way to confound his younger rival, and he hit back to win 4–6 6–2 6–4 6–4 and give the Czech Republic an unexpected early lead. "I'm not a guy who's going to shoot the other guy out of his pants with a hundred aces. I'm an all-court player who

uses his mind during the match, and I think I was smarter than him," said Stepanek, who returned to play Davis Cup three years ago with the express purpose of winning the trophy.

With world No. 37 Janko Tipsarevic set to face world No. 7 Tomas Berdych next, Serbia was staring at a 0–2 deficit on day one that almost certainly would have been too much to pull back. Sometime before the tie in an interview with www.daviscup.com, Nenad Zimonjic, Serbia's renowned doubles player, had remarked on how important it was that Tipsarevic had picked up his game again since getting injured in Toronto in August.

Raising his game for the big occasion is what Tipsarevic does best. If he could bring that level of performance to the court more often he would surely be a fixture in the top 20. His defeat of the American favorite Andy Roddick at the US Open could not have been better timed from a Davis Cup point of view. And as Zimonjic remarked, "All the Czech guys had a pretty bad US Open by their standards—they all lost in the first round."

That was particularly true of Berdych. The big, young Czech had had an unbelievable summer, reaching the semifinals of the French Open and the final of Wimbledon, beating Djokovic in the semis of the latter. Not surprisingly, perhaps, there was a definite drop-off in form soon afterward, and his defeat to Michael Llodra in New York was what many people in the game would call an "accident."

Before Djokovic's withdrawal, Tipsarevic had been preferred to Troicki for the No. 2 position on the basis that he had just beaten Roddick, and the American's game was not dissimilar to that of Berdych. The only difference, as it transpired, was that Roddick was nowhere near as wayward with his big weapon, the forehand, as Berdych was with his. Two sets had been forfeited before Berdych got his working, and by then he was left with a steep uphill task.

But when he broke Tipsarevic to lead 3–1 in the fourth, the Czech team could see him making the ascent. The Serb broke back immediately to stall him with a couple of inspired shots. The set eventually went to a tiebreak in which Tipsarevic soon took charge and, thanks to the galvanizing force of the crowd, ran out a 7–5 6–2 2–6 7–6(5) winner to level the tie. By Tipsarevic's own estimation, his victory over Roddick had been good "but not something unbelievable." This one, over another Top 10 player, however, clearly meant more to him.

Serbia is spoiled for choice when it comes to its doubles team. Zimonjic is the common denominator, but any one of three has partnered him in the past with success. However, after the way Tipsarevic played alongside the world No. 3 doubles player, against Croatia he would have been most people's favorite to get the nod. Instead—and no doubt to the delight of the home fans—Bogdan Obradovic, the Serbia captain, opted for Djokovic. Ultimately, it was both a wise and unsuccessful decision. Wise, because it gave Djokovic some badly needed court time after his illness as well as a feel for the occasion before the all-important reverse singles and, unsuccessful, because they lost.

Berdych and Stepanek are a formidable pairing—they have lost just once in eight rubbers—but the reason for their 3–6 6–1 6–4 6–1 victory seemed to have as much to do with their opponents' poor showing as their own intuitive understanding. Zimonjic attributed it to "a lack of concentration" but it seemed more like a case of the two Serbs simply not gelling—they were broken six times. Surprisingly, Zimonjic was the weakest link.

"I was expecting a lot better from myself, I wasn't returning well, and there were a lot of errors coming from my side," he said. "I kind of needed help, which meant I couldn't give Novak help, but maybe it wasn't a bad idea that he played today—he's had some match time, which could help him tomorrow."

Nevertheless, the doubles defeat meant that Serbia had to win both the remaining singles. "That's the goal, that's the only goal," said Djokovic. "There is no room for mistakes."

Indeed there weren't. Djokovic had all the motivation he needed to beat Berdych, although losing to him in the semifinals of Wimbledon during the summer would have been a small extra spur. An hour into the game, and with Berdych a set up, it was clear Djokovic was a completely different player than the one who had misfired against Tipsarevic. The tie was starting to take another nasty turn for the worse as far as the home nation was concerned.

And then Djokovic won a point, just a point, at 15–30 and 2–2 in the second set. Berdych hit a typically booming forehand, but Djokovic somehow managed to get a racket to it, scooping the ball back to the feet of the big Czech, who netted a volley. The Serb punched the air, and the home crowd suddenly had reason to believe again.

In the next game Djokovic even believed a smash was returnable. It wasn't, but worse still, he took a heavy tumble trying to achieve the impossible and

Pictured above:
Radek Stepanek (CZE);
Novak Djokovic (SRB)
receives treatment

Pictured clockwise from top right:

Tomas Berdych (CZE)

and Radek Stepanek (CZE);

The Serbian bench;

The Belgrade Arena

ended up lying motionless on his side before being helped to his chair, where his knee was bandaged. With that, Stepanek left the locker room and went courtside to be on hand for the celebrations just in case Djokovic retired. No such luck. Far from incapacitating Djokovic, the spill seemed to energize him. While the seven-minute delay seemed to have the opposite effect on Berdych.

There were mumblings about gamesmanship from the Czech side afterward, but given that the match appeared to be turning in Djokovic's favor just before the incident, it made no sense to deliberately interrupt proceedings. He did admit, though, that the fall "woke me up." There was little doubt that the momentum was now overwhelmingly with the Serb, who went on to win 4–6 6–3 6–2 6–4.

All Tipsarevic had to do now was keep upright as he rode the wave of euphoria that was now swilling around the Belgrade Arena. Easier said than done, of course. Tipsarevic managed it effortlessly for seven games before Stepanek finally got going. The second set went to a nervous tiebreak in which the Czech had the better chances. On set point, Stepanek was presented with a very makeable forehand but overhit it by the smallest of margins.

In such moments, ties, never mind rubbers, are won and lost, and this one most definitely was lost by the Czech Republic. Tipsarevic went on to win the set, and although Stepanek rallied from 5–1 down in the third to make a finale of it, the man from Belgrade had too much composure and confidence to falter now, winning 6–0 7–6(6) 6–4.

"Definitely the biggest Davis Cup tie of my life and maybe the biggest victory of my career," was how Tipsarevic summed it up. "These guys saved [Serbia from losing] in Davis Cup, each of them at least once. I have no idea how many matches Nenad has won for this country in doubles and I don't even want to talk about Novak. I'm just happy that for once I'm part of being, let's say, a small hero of the tie." ●

In fact, the most serious injury suffered by a player in those ties happened at the Luzhniki stadium, when the Czech Republic's Tomas Berdych rolled his ankle quite badly on the clay.

Not that the red stuff was always the preferred surface. On three occasions Russia chose carpet. They did for the 2006 final—mistakenly so, to Marat Safin's way of thinking. After the Russian No. 1 lost the second rubber in straight sets to David Nalbandian he complained that Shamil Tarpischev, the Russian captain, had chosen a surface that suited Nalbandian's game "perfectly" rather than his own. So it can't all be put down to the court type.

"I wish I could say there was some magical reason for it, but it could quite easily be just a coincidence," said Tursunov. "In the years I've played we've always faced guys there who were better on fast surfaces. Pretty much all the players were big hitters who didn't like clay—Andy Roddick, James Blake—people who didn't know how to play on it."

The only possible explanation for their great run had to be the quality and depth of the Russian team during those years—Safin's input cannot be underestimated—and the fact that they had a hugely experienced captain in Tarpischev.

While most countries are lucky if they can include two top class singles players in their team, Russia could usually name four, which meant that in the reverse singles it could bring in fresh players with little or no discernible difference to the overall standard. Nikolay Davydenko, Mikhail Youzhny, Igor Andreev, Tursunov, and, until his recent retirement, Safin have all been in the top 25 or higher, and at the start of Russia's fourteen-year run there was also, of course, Yevgeny Kafelnikov.

"I have definitely enjoyed playing there, but it's nerve-wracking playing at home—there's a lot of added pressure," said Tursunov. "At the same time it's rewarding, not necessarily rewarding for patriotic reasons, like I feel more Russian if I win and less Russian if I lose. I don't feel patriotism coming out of my pores just because I wrap myself in a flag, but it's definitely enjoyable for any athlete or person performing in anything when people are watching you and gaining enjoyment from it."

The crowd certainly motivated him in that unforgettable fourth rubber against Roddick in 2006, which earned Russia its place in the final. It was a perfect example of how Tarpischev was able to freshen things up. Safin and Youzhny had played in the opening day rubbers and given Russia a 2–0 lead, which the Americans then halved thanks to the Bryan brothers. Youzhny was now set to face Roddick, who had beaten him just a fortnight earlier at the US Open, but instead Tarpischev threw Tursunov into the mix and it worked.

The big, blonde Russian stormed into a two-sets-to-love lead only for Roddick to peg him back to two-all, which was when the rubber took on epic proportions. When Tursunov passed up on three match points in the twenty-fourth game of the fifth set, it looked as if he had missed his chance.

"I remember sitting in the chair during one of the changeovers and was kind of reflecting on the fact that had I known it was going to take so long to play that match I wouldn't have come out—I'd have called in sick that day!" joked Tursunov.

But it was worth the effort when he eventually prevailed after four hours and forty-nine minutes in a set that, at 17–15, equalled the longest in singles in World Group history, even if Messrs Isner and Mahut by then would have just been getting into their stride. Perhaps it was Baron Pierre de Coubertin's Olympic ideals that inspired the Russians: citius, altius, fortius—faster, higher, stronger. ●

CAPTAIN, MY CAPTAIN

To some it would seem the work of a Davis Cup captain is over once the teams have been nominated.
In fact, they are always on hand to offer support and encouragement while feeling every emotion on court.

Play-offs 17–19 September

		USA defeated Colombia 3–1 BOGOTA, COLOMBIA—OUTDOOR CLAY
		Austria defeated Israel 3–2 TEL AVIV, ISRAEL—INDOOR HARD
		Germany defeated South Africa 5–0 STUTTGART, GERMANY—OUTDOOR CLAY
		Sweden defeated Italy 3–2 LIDKOPING, SWEDEN—INDOOR HARD
		India defeated Brazil 3–2 CHENNAI, INDIA—OUTDOOR HARD
		Belgium defeated Australia 3–2 CAIRNS, AUSTRALIA—OUTDOOR HARD
		Kazakhstan defeated Switzerland 5–0 ASTANA, KAZAKHSTAN—INDOOR HARD
		Romania defeated Ecuador 5–0 BUCHAREST, ROMANIA—OUTDOOR CLAY

Introduction

The Davis Cup World Group lost some big names this year, one of them for good when, regrettably, United States's longest-serving captain, Patrick McEnroe, decided to retire to take up a position with the United States Tennis Association.

To the delight of everyone—the opposing Colombian team excluded, of course—he went out on a winning note, for which he had principally to thank one of his most faithful servants these past ten years. Mardy Fish secured three points for his captain, the first time an American had done so since Pete Sampras fifteen years ago.

Relegation from the World Group for the first time in twenty years would have been McEnroe's parting "gift" to the Americans had they lost in Bogota, but his great captaincy skills prevented that from happening. In the event, he made the contentious but ultimately correct decision to leave out Bob and Mike Bryan, arguably the best doubles team in the world these past five years, in favor of beefing up the singles.

"It truly was an honor to play for him," said Fish. "I saw him evolve from a rookie Davis Cup captain to a great Davis Cup captain, which is what he is now."

Another big name lost to the World Group—hopefully not for long—was Australia, which, to the surprise of many, was defeated at home by Belgium. The Belgians also had the temerity to knock the twenty-eight-time champions out of the World Group in 2007.

It would have been stretching a point to suggest that Lleyton Hewitt enjoyed mixed fortunes, but the tie proved a personal milestone for the twenty-nine-year-old Australian, who equalled the national record for Davis Cup victories after winning his opening singles rubber and then broke it when he and Paul Hanley won the doubles in straight sets to give him his forty-fourth victory in the old competition.

Even Australia's defeat didn't resonate quite as loudly around the world as news of Switzerland's 5–0 loss to Kazakhstan. Roger Federer, the former world No. 1, may have been conspicuous by his absence, but it was an alarming result nonetheless.

Elsewhere, Leander Paes had cause for celebration both on and off the court after India came back from 2–0 down for the first time in history to defeat Brazil and the mercurial thirty-seven-year-old was honored at an official dinner in recognition of his twenty years of Davis Cup duty. Sweden had a scare but held on to its World Group status for an eleventh consecutive year, largely thanks to world No. 5 Robin Soderling, the only Swede ranked in the top 300 in singles. ●

United States v Colombia

Patrick McEnroe could have asked for an easier match in which to bow out as the longest serving Davis Cup captain for the United States. The last time an American team played in Bogota, Colombia, in 1974, it was soundly beaten 4–1. In 2010 there was every chance that the altitude and pressureless balls would conspire to make a mockery of the rankings once again.

Furthermore, there was the stress of knowing that defeat would relegate the United States from the World Group for the first time in twenty years. Ten years' experience as captain was drawn heavily upon by McEnroe as he contemplated his lineup. He ultimately took the unprecedented step of omitting the best doubles team in the world, the Bryan

brothers, from his selection. It was a choice that could easily have backfired.

McEnroe felt that because of the draining climate he might need three singles players in his team of four rather than the usual two, which meant leaving out Mike and Bob Bryan. A key factor in that decision was the form, fitness, and, not least, the versatility of Mardy Fish, a player who has been surplus to requirements in Davis Cup more often than he cares to remember, as he noted when commenting on McEnroe's qualities as a captain.

"He always was really straightforward. Sometimes brutally straightforward as far as where I stood, and I respected that."

This season, however, Fish was finally fulfilling some of the potential that many saw in him as early as the start of the millennium. He reached four finals in the summer, including the Cincinnati Masters, winning two of them. He did not let his captain down. In the event, he became the first American to win all three points since Pete Sampras in 1995, spending a total of eleven hours on court, and playing fourteen sets.

"The key for Mardy all weekend was his mental toughness," said McEnroe. "Because he is so physically fit now he has become mentally much stronger."

He needed that mental strength from day one as Colombia's No. 2, Alejandro Falla, pushed him to the limits. Colombia's tactic was to keep the ball in play and basically wear its opponents down in the thin air circulating in the Plaza de Toros, a converted bullring (the hosts got the idea of playing in it from Spain, who had thrashed United States at a similar venue in Madrid in the 2008 semifinals).

Fish eventually came through a match of many ups and downs to win 4–6 6–1 6–4 3–6 6–4. But Colombia's response was impressive. Santiago Giraldo was ranked forty-two places beneath Sam Querrey, the American No. 2, but he flouted the discrepancy, playing like a man inspired, to win 6–2 6–4 7–5 and square the tie.

McEnroe had named Ryan Harrison to partner John Isner in the doubles but was probably always thinking he might play Fish alongside Isner, providing the former recovered from his singles in time, which he did. Davis Cup debutant Robert Farah and Carlos Salamanca gave it their all but pulled up a little short,

losing 6–4 6–4 6–7(5) 6–3. "I always knew that Mardy Fish is a great doubles player, but I was surprised just how hard John Isner served," said Farah. "I mean, there were some balls that I could not even see."

Fish could not find his rhythm in the first set on day three against Giraldo, but as McEnroe put it: "He can adapt to the situation and go to his toolbox as needed." Even so, it was the Colombian who almost stole the match at five-all in the fifth, when he broke the American, prompting the home fans to chant: "Yes, he can. Yes, he can." Actually, no he couldn't.

"All during the match, I told him to think about the sacrifice and hard work that he has put in over the ten months," said McEnroe. "And on that changeover, I said, 'keep believing.'"

He needed to be a big believer because, although Fish broke straight back, the Colombian had three break points in Fish's next service game before the American doggedly came through the ordeal to win 3–6 6–3 7–5 4–6 8–6 in four hours and five minutes.

The United States's World Group status had been preserved for another year, and McEnroe went out on a high with his seventeenth Davis Cup win as captain, just one fewer than the American record held by Tom Gorman. ●

Pictured above:

Santiago Giraldo (COL)

Pictured below:

Team USA

sets—it was his forty-fifth Davis Cup rubber and Adrian Ungur's second.

But the tide was already turning before the end of the second set, and Ungur began nibbling away at Lapentti's advantage. By the fourth set the Ecuadorian's body language alone was an open invitation to his opponent to press on with his attack.

When Gloria Gaynor's "I Will Survive" was played during one changeover, it seemed to be sending a

message more to the visiting Ecuadorian than the home player, but with Ungur's drop shots sapping the energy from Lapentti's legs, there was no way the Ecuadorian was going to survive.

On the eve of the action, Hanescu, the Ecuadorian No. 1, had spoken about how he hoped to win his first match "easily" in order to stay fresh for the rest of the weekend. Well, he got his wish, beating Ivan Endara— playing in his first live Davis Cup rubber—6–2 6–2 6–2 in just one hour forty-nine minutes. When the six-foot, six-inch Hanescu is getting in 84 percent of his first serves he's a handful for anyone, nevermind a Davis Cup rookie. "I used the kick serve a lot, which was good, as he's a short guy," he said.

As it turned out, Nicolas Lapentti wasn't even fit enough to play in the doubles, so his brother was partnered by Endara. It was a tall order for them in more ways than one against Hanescu and the shorter six-foot, four-inch Tecau. The latter has been busily making a name for himself on the doubles circuit, winning five titles this year, and in harness with Hanescu powered to a 6–2 6–2 6–2 win. To make matters worse, even the dead rubbers proved beyond Ecuador's capabilities. ●

Estadio Rafael Osuna, Mexico City, Mexico

For a man who was as much loved as Rafael Osuna there is never a good time to go. Yet it was appropriate that his last performance as a tennis player in 1969, shortly before meeting an untimely death in a plane crash at the age of thirty, was to almost single-handedly defeat Australia in a Davis Cup tie, something that Mexico had not managed in eleven previous attempts, nor since.

According to his closest friend and longtime doubles partner, Antonio Palafox, Osuna was obsessed with beating the Australians. "In some place, on some occasion, I'm going to beat them," he would tell him.

That place eventually turned out to be the famous Chapultepec Club in Mexico City, which,

after his death, was renamed the Estadio Rafael Osuna. He was greatly mourned. The little Mexican may not have won as many Grand Slams as famous Australians like Rod Laver and Margaret Court, but he was no less deserving of the posthumous award that was bestowed on him when, like them, a stadium was named after him.

Osuna didn't have a Roy Emerson or a Ken Rosewall to push him on to greater heights, as Laver had in his own country. Mexican tennis virtually began and ended with Osuna. He was often described as ubiquitous—he needed to be to keep alive the hopes of his nation in Davis Cup and Grand Slams.

While his only Grand Slam title, the US Open in 1963, was a fitting testimony to his talents, it was in

Davis Cup that he experienced some of his most memorable moments. Every year—for the last five that he was alive—he told the Mexican Federation that it would be his last in the competition, but whenever his country came calling he could never resist the challenge. How apt that he eventually realized his goal just twelve days before his death in a Mexican Airlines crash near Monterey that killed seventy-nine. He left a wife, Leslie, and a six-month old son named Rafael Jr.

Mexico's fate could not have been in better hands going into that fifth and final rubber against Australia. Osuna had won his opening singles rubber against Ray Ruffels, as well as the doubles alongside Vicente Zarazua, when he took his third point of the tie by beating Bill Bowrey 6–2 3–6 8–6 6–3 to give Mexico victory. Coincidentally, it was not only Osuna's last match but also that of another great man, Australian captain Harry Hopman, who retired.

At long last, Osuna had gained his revenge on the Aussies. The Mexicans had suffered at Australian hands enough, most painfully in 1962 when they lost in the Davis Cup final in Brisbane 5–0. Their run to that final began with a famous 3–2 victory against the United States at Chapultepec, when Osuna, typically, won both his singles rubbers, including a straight-sets defeat of his good friend, Chuck McKinley, who the following year would win the Wimbledon title.

Born into a family of intellectuals, Osuna was said, by his friend Palafox, to be wise beyond his years. He played the game with a disarming smile through eyes with thick lashes and was universally loved, although Palafox said he sometimes used the smile to disguise his anger.

Playing chiefly during the years before the Open Era, he was ranked in the top ten from 1962 to 1964 and in the year of his Grand Slam triumph he was No. 1. He was once offered $100,000 by the promoter Jack Kramer to turn professional but turned it down. "He's the most spectacular player I've seen in years," said Kramer. "He could make a fortune, but he won't do it—I don't understand the Mexican."

To the surprise of some, the great Fred Perry even included Osuna among his top five of all time. "Rafael Osuna is speed, speed, speed," said Perry.

"His service isn't particularly good, nor is his forehand very powerful—although his volley is stupendous—but he has the fastest hands and feet I've ever seen. Without doubt he is one of the five best tennis players of all time."

The pinnacle of Osuna's career was unquestionably the US Open final which he won in straight sets with a quite brilliant tactical performance against the big-serving American Frank Froehling III. Walter Bingham, of Sports Illustrated, thought Osuna took advantage of the fact that on a hot day many men in the stadium had taken off their jackets, "leaving a panorama of white shirts as a background for lobs."

Another American writer, Bud Collins, wrote: "Osuna cleverly neutralized [Froehling's] power with wonderfully conceived and executed tactics, especially lobbed service returns from ten to twelve feet behind the baseline. In fact, Osuna climbed the wall of the stadium to retrieve smashes and float back perfect lobs, frustrating Froehling with his nimble speed around the court, touch, and tactical variations."

The best Osuna could manage at Wimbledon was a quarterfinal, but he won the doubles there twice: first in 1960 with Dennis Ralston, his longtime friend from University of Southern California days, when they beat the British pair, Mike Davies and Bobby Wilson; and again in 1963 when he and Palafox beat Pierre Darmon and Jean Claude Barclay of France.

He was inducted into the Hall of Fame in 1979.

THE COLOURS OF THE CROWD

There is nothing quite like a Davis Cup tie to bring a crowd to life. Whether cheering on the home side or trying
to boost the away team, the fans play a vital role in making Davis Cup tennis matches unique for all involved.

Final 3-5 December

Serbia defeated France 3-2 BELGRADE, SERBIA-INDOOR HARD

DAVIS CUP TEAM SERBIA
JELISAVČIĆ

The Final

Serbia v France

With a Serb having won not one Grand Slam title but two, people have become a bit blasé about Serbia's success in tennis. It took the likeable Janko Tipsarevic, who is articulate in a language that is not his own, to offer some perspective when asked before the final just how much of an achievement it would be if Serbia were to win the Davis Cup by BNP Paribas.

"It's not Spain playing in the final or the States, which they do every four or five years, or Russia, this is Serbia," he said, bursting with pride at the accomplishment of a country with a population of just eight million.

No one has done more to improve Serbia's reputation abroad since the Yugoslav Wars than its tennis players, and Tipsarevic is one of its finest ambassadors.

"If you look at all the political differences and everything that happened to the country, and then ten years after we are in a position to win Davis Cup—even three years back we didn't have one hard court in the country—it is just something so shocking, and I think it should be shocking to everyone, not just us."

At risk of falling out with two of his fellow Serbs who won those Grand Slam titles—Novak Djokovic and Ana Ivanovic—Tipsarevic made the valid point that the country would possibly relate more to a team success than an individual one.

"I would guess that Serbians would maybe appreciate more if the country does something apart from the individual, but maybe I'm wrong," he said. "I'm not saying that winning Davis Cup is bigger than winning a Grand Slam. It's really tough to compare because one is a team competition and the other is an individual competition, but for sure it's going to be the biggest news that Serbia has had in a long, long time."

And it was. Anyone who was at the Belgrade Arena on December 3–5—or anywhere else in Serbia, for that matter—could not have failed to recognize the sense of pride and joy sweeping the nation when it actually did win the old trophy in a thrilling and historic final against the nine-time champion, France.

In fact, they could not have celebrated more wildly had they won the World Cup. Football may remain the country's most popular sport, but it's at basketball, handball, volleyball, water polo, and now tennis that its teams excel.

The old country of Yugoslavia may never have won Davis Cup, but in the space of five years, two of its young republics, Croatia and Serbia, have won the most prestigious team competition in tennis—both in their first appearances in the final.

While Serbia may have been the favorite to win this final, partly because of the importance of home advantage in Davis Cup, its players spent the entire weekend playing catch-up. But never once did they give up believing that they could do it. When they eventually did get their noses in front, in the fifth and final rubber, they pulled away almost effortlessly from the opposition to become the not-so-unlucky thirteenth winner of this famous trophy.

In the opinion of many, Bogdan Obradovic, the Serbian captain, had taken a major gamble by replacing the more experienced Tipsarevic with Viktor Troicki. However, it proved to be an inspired decision, because Troicki chose this of all days to play the best tennis of his life, beating Michael Llodra, one of the outstanding players of this Davis Cup season, in straight sets 6–2 6–2 6–3.

Normally, players who are substituted in finals, whatever the sport, and then see their teammates go on to achieve glory are a touch subdued in their celebrations, but not Tipsarevic, who rejoiced as enthusiastically as anyone. Since the start of the season, when Serbia beat the United States, there was a strong sense of camaraderie running through this team.

When Tipsarevic said that he didn't care if he didn't play in the final so long as Serbia won, he meant it. And as disappointed as he was by his performance in the opening rubber against Gael Monfils, he knew his contribution to this overall victory was unquestioned. Without his heroics in the semifinals, when he won both his singles rubbers against Czech Republic, Serbia would never have made it to the final.

"We have to say that this was a friendship that won the title," said No. 1 player Djokovic. "Not just between us players but the whole team that was backstage that people don't know about—the physios, the fitness coaches, the stringers, the team managers—everybody has done a great job."

As a result, each and every one of them—including the president of the Serbian Tennis Federation, Slobodan Zivojinovic—kept their promise that if they won the trophy they would have their heads shaved on court. Djokovic, he of the Busby top, had the most to lose, but it seemed a small price to pay for taking the scalp of France. In time Obradovic might even thank them since the shearing seemed to take years off him.

It was debatable which was the more severe: the looks of Djokovic and company, who, as barbers like to say, looked as if they had had their hair cut with a knife and fork, or the straight-sets beatings of Monfils and Llodra. Two-one up going into the final day, Guy Forget, the France captain, must have been quietly confident of taking the one point his side needed for victory.

The truth is they were taken aback by Serbia's determination to keep its appointment with destiny while driven on by the support of a fervent capacity crowd of 16,200 (minus, of course, about 1,400 marvelous French fans) that reached a deafening crescendo for those last two rubbers. The city of Belgrade has had a fortress on and off since the first century; the Belgrade Arena, where Serbia remained unbeaten, is its second.

The absence of France's No. 1, Jo-Wilfried Tsonga, who snapped a tendon in his troublesome knee a

Pictured below:

Janko Tipsarevic (SRB);
The French bench awaits
the result of a challenge

Pictured opposite:
Gael Monfils (FRA)

month before the final, proved crucial, although Forget, to his credit, did not harp on about it.

"They gave everything they had," he said of his team. "We had rough times when Jo-Wilfried was injured, and obviously things could have been a little different if he had played the final, but the rest of the boys were wonderful. All the way until the Sunday we believed the win was possible.

"Unfortunately, the Serbs were too good—Novak was as good as he can be and Troicki was unbelievable with his returns against Llodra, who is probably playing the best tennis of his life right now. That we didn't expect.

"We look sad now because we're going to leave Belgrade with a small trophy and a lot of fatigue and sadness in our eyes, but overall we have to look at it in a very positive way that this group [of players] is young and has great potential and, with a leader like Jo, the team in the future will be even better."

The fact is Tsonga had not played for them since the first-round match against Germany, when he had to retire injured. The more destabilizing loss was probably that of Julien Benneteau, who had to withdraw from the final just a fortnight before with a wrist injury. He had been unbeaten in four rubbers during the season. But if any country can cope with such losses it is France, whose strength in depth is the envy of the world.

Besides, there seemed an element of sweet justice in the promotion of Arnaud Clement to the team because he had missed out on France's last two appearances in the final, in 2001 when it won, and 2002, when it lost. Also, Monfils had been displaying greater maturity since being asked to fill Tsonga's rather large shoes, winning all three of his singles rubbers, including the crucial one on the opening day against Argentina's David Nalbandian in the semifinal.

Forget had a slight dig at the opposition when he said: "These guys have been able to make the finals without Jo. I don't know if Serbia could have gone to the finals without Novak. On the other hand, Spain, which is a good example, won Davis Cup without Rafael Nadal when they went to Buenos Aires to beat Argentina. That was a great effort. That's when you realize how strong a team can be, when you can miss one of your best players and still be very competitive."

Be that as it may, the Serbian team looked strong. Even that great favorite of Paris crowds, Ilie Nastase, who won the 1973 French Open, thought that the Serbs would win, but then he would; he is a close friend of Zivojinovic. But it was hard to argue with his reasoning.

"Serbia's captain Bogdan Obradovic has young, yet experienced players at his disposal, who are unlikely to be shaken by the pressure of the moment," said Nastase. "I am certain they will find a way to battle the pressure. Besides, they will have the crowd on their side."

Much was being made of the pressure that Monfils would be under to get France off to a winning start, but the young Parisian handled himself as nimbly in the press conference as he does on a tennis court, cleverly turning the tables on the opposition, when he remarked: "He [Tipsarevic] will be very nervous because he plans to come out first on the court in front of the Serbian crowd. It will be tough for him. I will try to be very relaxed and just play my game.

"I practiced all these days for this moment, to feel the pressure I have right now. I'm really looking forward to tomorrow. It will be a good experience, and then I will be happy to share [it] with you."

And that is exactly what happened: Tipsarevic was as nervous as Monfils was relaxed. The pair had had a tough match against each other at the US Open three months earlier, when the Frenchman emerged the winner in four sets, after which the Serb had played his blinder against Czech Republic. He beat the new world No. 7, Tomas Berdych, in four sets in the second rubber and then the Czech talisman Radek Stepanek in straight sets in the decisive fifth rubber.

But by his own admission, he had not played well since then. His game is flawed by inconsistency. Perhaps it was because of his honeymoon following his wedding in July to the beautiful Serbian TV presenter Biljana Sesevic. He had been teased with questions about it beforehand, and at the press conference was asked whether he felt different now.

"In what way? Do I look more pretty or how," Tipsarevic replied with his usual good humor.

"Are you more confident?" asked his inquirer.

Unusually for Tipsarevic, it was a teammate who came back first with the quip.

"He's undefeated in the Davis Cup since he got

Pictured below:

Viktor Troicki (SRB) and
Nenad Zimonjic (SRB);
Michael Llodra (FRA) and
Arnaud Clement (FRA);
Viktor Troicki (SRB)

married," interrupted Nenad Zimonjic.

"That's more pressure for the French," added Tipsarevic just for good measure.

But just as Monfils had forecast, the pressure was all Serbia's, as was evident from the successive pair of double faults with which Tipsarevic opened—"this never happened to me [before] in my life." He hadn't played since losing to Roger Federer in Basel a month earlier and it showed.

Tipsarevic had a 3–2 advantage in head-to-heads but you would never have guessed it from this match. "Having a guy like Gael, well, he doesn't attack that much, but he doesn't give you a lot of unforced errors," he said. "Just having this, we say, like a worm in your head, that you have to win by yourself every point, it was difficult for me today."

The surprisingly emphatic nature of the 6–1 7–6(4) 6–0 scoreline suggested that he may not have lost only this match but also his place in the final rubber. The French fans barely had time to enjoy the victory before Djokovic, as befitting a team leader, was moving to an early break advantage in the second rubber against Gilles Simon, who had, a little surprisingly, been chosen over Llodra.

Whether that was because the court was much slower than the one at Paris Bercy, where Llodra had sensationally beaten Djokovic in straight sets the previous month, or because the thirty-year-old's form and mental state were in question since arriving in Belgrade, no one was sure.

Amelie Mauresmo, who was in Belgrade as both a supporter of French tennis and in particular of Llodra, whom she had helped coach with some success since the summer, suspected that he was being held back for what could have been a decisive final rubber. Whatever the reason, it was unlikely that a steady Eddy

Pictured above:

Novak Djokovic (SRB);
Michael Llodra (FRA) is
consoled by his teammates

Pictured opposite:

Nenad Zimonjic (SRB)

week had ended an incredibly successful partnership with Canada's Daniel Nestor by winning the Barclays ATP World Tour title in London. As luck would have it, his new partner is going to be Llodra, which would add some spice to the third rubber.

As it happened, Obradovic went for Zimonjic and Troicki, who reached the final of the ATP World Team Championship in Dusseldorf earlier in the year but perhaps even more impressively scored Serbia's only point against Spain when they lost to the eventual champions in 2009.

For three-and-a-half sets of easily the most exciting rubber of the weekend it looked like a great decision. The French pair was surprisingly slow off the mark and Clement, the late replacement, was successfully being targeted as the weak link by the Serbs.

The crowd, who had been uncharacteristically subdued on the first day, now found its voice—too much so to the French way of thinking and that of the Spanish umpire, Enric Molina, who, in apparently very good Serbian, repeatedly asked them to keep quiet while the players were serving.

One time he wisely enlisted the help of the Serbian team, having already told the crowd: "Ladies and gentlemen, look at your players. Nenad and Viktor are asking you to be silent." Tipsarevic then took the microphone and repeated the request. The upshot was that Serbia was able to recover its composure in the second-set tiebreak and forge to a two-sets-to-love lead.

"When you have a big event like this, you always have twenty or thirty idiots that are whistling every time you toss the ball," Forget told the Serbian media. "That's very frustrating. It's very unfair. These people don't need to be on a sport field anywhere. I think that kind of spoiled the pleasure that you can have on the court because you're always fighting the chair umpire to apply the rules. I hope in the future, you will be able to get rid of these people, because most of the people were wonderful."

Although France won the third set with an isolated break, Serbia still looked like favorites to win the rubber right up until the eighth game of the fourth set. When holding a 4–3 lead, they missed two break-point opportunities that would have left them serving for the

like Simon was going to cut it against Djokovic. Having been No. 7 in the world in 2008, the man from Nice had now slipped to No. 42. For all its depth, France lacked a viable No. 2 for this final.

Monfils had expressed the hope that winning the opening rubber would put more pressure on "Nole." The only possible pressure the world No. 3 would have felt was from the handshake Simon gave him before the start, after which he exerted a firm grip on the game that he did not release until the 6–3 6–1 7–5 victory was complete and the tie was all square.

It looked like the doubles would, as ever, be key. After all, history said so. Only three nations—Australia (1977), Russia (2002), and Spain (2004)—had ever lost the doubles in a final and gone on to win the trophy since the Challenge Round was abolished in 1972. Winning it, though, might not have been a good omen for France, the team on the receiving end in 2002.

The French team of Llodra and Clement virtually picked itself since they had been playing doubles together for six years and had a 7–2 record in Davis Cup ties, but there were about half a dozen possible permutations for the Serbian team. The most intriguing question of all was whether or not Djokovic would be kept in reserve for the reverse singles.

Tipsarevic and Trocki had partnered each other at the St. Petersburg Open in October— could that be a clue? Surely, Obradovic would not leave out Zimonjic, the world No. 3 doubles player, who only the previous match—not to mention a stranglehold on the tie.

Instead France held serve and their nerve and began to grow in confidence, notably little Clement. The thirty-two-year-old was suddenly inspired. He needed to be because Llodra was having a torrid time. It was fortunate for them that Troicki wasn't much better, but it was a great comeback all the same and the 3–6 6–7(3) 6–4 7–5 6–4 win put France in the driving seat.

"Arnaud helped me a lot," said Llodra. "That's the difference when you play with one of your best friends. Sometimes when you play with someone else, you can't find the good words at the good moment. Today he helped me a lot."

Forget concurred: "Had they not been friends, have this really strong relationship together, there was no way they could have come back and win that match. I think a doubles team is like a couple. You go through storms together, but eventually you're very proud that your relation[ship] goes for a long time and you're able to achieve wonderful things."

Watching the match was Fabrice Santoro, who was covering the tie for France radio. He was a member of the French team that beat Russia in the doubles eight years ago, when they also came from behind, a fact he was happy to bring to the attention of Marat Safin. The recently retired Russian, by chance, was commentating for Davis Cup radio in an adjoining booth, and he was even happier to remind the little Frenchman of how that final eventually turned out.

No one would wish Paul-Henri Mathieu's experience on anyone—let alone remind him of it—but this tie was now clearly heading for a fifth and final rubber denouement, which meant someone was going to suffer much like the poor Frenchman, who was just twenty at the time. Hopefully, not as acutely, because Mathieu lost a two-sets-to-love lead against Russia's Mikhail Youzhny and with it, of course, the chance of sporting immortality.

After the way Llodra and Troicki had played, it was anyone's guess who would have that unenviable task, but first, of course, Djokovic had to overcome Monfils. Judging by the young Frenchman's form on the first day that wasn't going to be easy even if Djokovic was unbeaten against him in five previous meetings.

In the event, it was that easy (well, from our cozy

armchair perspective it was, anyway). Of course, the pressure upon Djokovic must have been enormous, but you would never have guessed it from his performance. If Monfils was like a cat, according to Tipsarevic, on the opening day Djokovic was like a tiger, pouncing on anything short. He never gave the Frenchman a moment's respite and pounded his way to a 6–2 6–2 6–4 victory.

Afterward Djokovic revealed that he was human, after all. "I was very focused, of course, very motivated," he said, "but I felt a lot of pressure, 1–2 down, third day against Gael who hasn't lost a match this year in Davis Cup. He's been playing unbelievable, so under the circumstances I played maybe the best tennis this year."

No sooner had his match finished than he took on the role of cheerleader. All through this tie he had spoken of the need for the Serbian fans to get behind the team and cheer them home, and now as they went into the deciding rubber he urged the fans over the public address system to drown what he described as "a professional and organized" French support.

The two captains now had to make selection decisions that would define their season, possibly their career in the case of Obradovic. Forget, of course, has

Pictured above:
Viktor Troicki (SRB) is held aloft;
Serbia captain Bogdan Obradovic

Pictured above:
Serbia lifts the trophy;
Novak Djokovic (SRB)

already won the Davis Cup, twice as a player and once as a captain, as well as the Fed Cup. Both decided to change their original nominations.

"We believe that Viktor is a good option," said Djokovic. "Unfortunately, Janko in this moment, he's not ready enough to perform his best. He didn't play well in the first match. But that's why we are a team here and that's why we have options."

Forget had no other option really than to go for the serve-and-volley player, Llodra; Simon would have been far too much of a risk, even though his end-of-season form had been encouraging. Either way it would probably have made no difference: Troicki was that good. It was probably of little consolation to Llodra as he sobbed uncontrollably into his towel at the finish while comforted by his captain and teammates.

"Obviously, you could tell me now that it was the wrong decision," said Forget. "But I still believed when I had to take my decision last night that that was our best chance. What I didn't expect was Viktor to be so good."

Remember, this was a man who three months earlier had come within a few points of prematurely ending his teammate Djokovic's interest at the US Open. It was credited by some for provoking the latter's excellent rush of form toward the end of the season that carried on into this final. So that was another reason for the Serbs to be grateful to the twenty-four-year-old Troicki. Unlike the unfortunate Mathieu, he did find sporting immortality. ●

Player of the Year: Novak Djokovic

Born May 22 1987 in Belgrade, Serbia
Turned professional 2003

After the way Viktor Troicki performed in the fifth rubber of the Davis Cup by BNP Paribas final, Guy Forget may have had second thoughts about the wisdom of his suggestion that Serbia was a one-man team. Come to think of it, after what Janko Tipsarevic achieved for the country in the semifinal round it's surprising he made the inference in the first place.

According to Don Shula, the famous American football coach, "the one-man team is a complete and total myth." Those who saw the Diego Maradona–inspired Argentina win the 1986 World Cup might beg to differ, but the broad principle is hard to argue against. No sport, these past six or seven years, has possessed a more outstanding individual than Roger Federer, but, for all his talent, the best he and his Swiss teammates have been able to manage in tennis's premier team competition so far is the semifinals.

To his credit, throughout the competition, Djokovic has emphasized that Serbia's success was the result of teamwork—and he wasn't just talking about the four men who stepped onto the court. In fact, in the final he went one step further and suggested it was borne out of friendship.

Every competition must have a Player of the Year, and for the Davis Cup in 2010, it had to be Djokovic, who was unbeaten in seven singles rubbers. It probably would have been all eight but for an attack of acute gastroenteritis prior to his scheduled match against Radek Stepanek in the semifinals; after all, he had beaten the Czech Republic player four times out of five.

It was his leadership qualities as much as his individual excellence that carried Serbia to glory. Never was that more evident than in the reverse singles in the final against Gael Monfils when, with his team trailing 2–1, the pressure on him to keep his country in contention must have been crippling, and yet he seemed to make light of the burden. A show of character like that just had to have rubbed off on Troicki going into the last rubber.

There is a strong sense of nationalistic pride coursing through the veins of most Serbian sportsmen and -women, no doubt heightened by the Yugoslav Wars, and it's particularly evident in tennis players like Djokovic.

"When you have this opportunity to play for your country and feel the team spirit, it's something you cannot describe with words," he said after the victory that made Serbia first believe that the impossible was, in fact, achievable: the defeat of multiple-champion United States in the first round.

Sometimes players get out of the Davis Cup what they put into it, and Djokovic put in a Herculean effort. It was only fitting that he got his rewards. He was the only one of the world's top four who played in every round in which their country competed, but more than that—and what many people don't appreciate—is that each of his efforts in the four rounds took place almost immediately after extended runs in tournament play.

The nine sets of singles required in March to put down the challenge of the two giant Americans, Sam Querrey and John Isner, may have had something to do with the fact that just five days earlier Djokovic had won the final in Dubai.

Similarly, the dazzling tennis that stunned two of Croatia's finest, Marin Cilic and Ivan Ljubicic, and eventually silenced their fanatical supporters in Split in July, came just a week after reaching the semifinals of Wimbledon. And that was on top of a tricky change in playing surface, too.

Likewise, six days after a memorable US Open final in September and a tough loss to Rafael Nadal, Djokovic had avenged that All England Club defeat to Tomas Berdych, squaring the semifinal in Belgrade—even with an upset tummy. And last, the final and another massive two-point contribution from wins against Gilles Simon and Monfils, which came six days after reaching the last four of the Barclays ATP World Tour Finals.

Of course, there have been some hard losses along the way. Like the double defeat to the Belgians—Olivier Rochus and Kristof Vliegen—in 2004 when he was a mere seventeen years old, and another more painful double whammy against Spain in 2009, when both David Ferrer and Rafael Nadal beat him in straight sets.

Yet all the while there has been no real evidence of his individual career suffering because he has answered the call of his country, even if he has still to add another Grand Slam to his 2008 Australian Open title. He was world No. 3 at the start of 2010, and despite some illness earlier in the season, he was still world No. 3 at the start of 2011. It's just a matter of prioritizing, and most would say that, so far, Djokovic has got his priorities just right. ●

AND FINALLY...

All eyes might have been on the thrilling action that unfolded on court at the Belgrade Arena for the Davis Cup by BNP Paribas final, but there was plenty happening off the court too.

WORLD GROUP

First Round 5-7 March
Spain defeated Switzerland 4-1. Logrono, ESP, Clay (I): Stanislas Wawrinka (SUI) d. Nicolas Almagro (ESP) 36 64 36 75 63; David Ferrer (ESP) d. Marco Chiudinelli (SUI) 62 76(5) 61; Marcel Granollers/Tommy Robredo (ESP) d. Yves Allegro/Stanislas Wawrinka (SUI) 76(8) 62 46 64; David Ferrer (ESP) d. Stanislas Wawrinka (SUI) 62 64 60; Nicolas Almagro (ESP) d. Marco Chiudinelli (SUI) 61 63.

France defeated Germany 4-1, Toulon, FRA, Hard (I): Gael Monfils (FRA) d. Philipp Kohlschreiber (GER) 61 64 76(5); Jo-Wilfried Tsonga (FRA) d. Benjamin Becker (GER) 63 62 67(2) 63; Julien Benneteau/Michael Llodra (FRA) d. Christopher Kas/Philipp Kohlschreiber (GER) 61 64 16 75; Simon Greul (GER) d. Jo-Wilfried Tsonga (FRA) 46 62 10 ret.; Julien Benneteau (FRA) d. Benjamin Becker (GER) 62 75.

Russia defeated India 3-2, Moscow, RUS, Hard (I): Igor Kunitsyn (RUS) d. Somdev Devvarman (IND) 67(6) 76(4) 63 64; Mikhail Youzhny (RUS) d. Rohan Bopanna (IND) 64 62 63; Mahesh Bhupathi/Leander Paes (IND) d. Teimuraz Gabashvili/Igor Kunitsyn (RUS) 63 62 62; Mikhail Youzhny (RUS) d. Somdev Devvarman (IND) 62 61 63; Rohan Bopanna (IND) d. Teimuraz Gabashvili (RUS) 76(5) 64.

Argentina defeated Sweden 3-2, Stockholm, SWE, Hard (I): Robin Soderling (SWE) d. Eduardo Schwank (ARG) 61 76(0) 75; Leonardo Mayer (ARG) d. Joachim Johansson (SWE) 57 63 75 64; David Nalbandian/Horacio Zeballos (ARG) d. Robert Lindstedt/Robin Soderling (SWE) 62 76(4) 76(5); Robin Soderling (SWE) d. Leonardo Mayer (ARG) 75 76(5) 75; David Nalbandian (ARG) d. Andreas Vinciguerra (SWE) 75 63 46 64.

Croatia defeated Ecuador 5-0, Varazdin, CRO, Hard (I): Ivo Karlovic (CRO) d. Nicolas Lapentti (ECU) 62 57 67(2) 63 64; Marin Cilic (CRO) d. Giovanni Lapentti (ECU) 64 63 63; Marin Cilic/Ivo Karlovic (CRO) d. Giovanni Lapentti/Nicolas Lapentti (ECU) 76(3) 63 75; Antonio Veic (CRO) d. Julio-Cesar Campozano (ECU) 64 76(4); Ivan Dodig (CRO) d. Ivan Endara (ECU) 61 63.

Serbia defeated USA 3-2, Belgrade, SRB, Clay (I): Viktor Troicki (SRB) d. John Isner (USA) 76(4) 67(5) 75 64; Novak Djokovic (SRB) d. Sam Querrey (USA) 62 76(4) 26 63; Bob Bryan/John Isner (USA) d. Janko Tipsarevic/Nenad Zimonjic (SRB) 76(8) 57 76(8) 63; Novak Djokovic (SRB) d. John Isner (USA) 75 36 63 67(6) 64; Sam Querrey (USA) d. Viktor Troicki (SRB) 75 62.

Czech Republic defeated Belgium 4-1, Bree, BEL, Clay (I): Tomas Berdych (CZE) d. Olivier Rochus (BEL) 63 60 64; Radek Stepanek (CZE) d. Xavier Malisse (BEL) 62 64 76(3); Tomas Berdych/Radek Stepanek (CZE) d. Steve Darcis/Olivier Rochus (BEL) 76(0) 60 63; Steve Darcis (BEL) d. Jan Hajek (CZE) 76(6) 16 64; Lukas Dlouhy (CZE) d. Christophe Rochus (BEL) 16 76(3) 75.

Chile defeated Israel 4-1, Coquimbo, CHI, Clay (U): Nicolas Massu (CHI) d. Dudi Sela (ISR) 46 62 62 64; Fernando Gonzalez (CHI) d. Harel Levy (ISR) 26 63 64 64; Jonathan Erlich/Andy Ram (ISR) d. Jorge Aguilar/Paul Capdeville (CHI) 67(5) 76(9) 26 61 60; Fernando Gonzalez (CHI) d. Dudi Sela (ISR) 64 64 63; Jorge Aguilar (CHI) d. Harel Levy (ISR) 76(3) 61.

Quarterfinals 9-11 July
France defeated Spain 5-0, Clermont-Ferrand, FRA, Hard (I): Gael Monfils (FRA) d. David Ferrer (ESP) 76(3) 62 46 57 64; Michael Llodra (FRA) d. Fernando Verdasco (ESP) 67(5) 64 63 76(2); Julien Benneteau/Michael Llodra (FRA) d. Feliciano Lopez/Fernando Verdasco (ESP) 61 62 67(6) 76(5); Gilles Simon (FRA) d. Nicolas Almagro (ESP) 76(4) 76(7); Julien Benneteau (FRA) d. Feliciano Lopez (ESP) 76(3) 64.

Argentina defeated Russia 3-2, Moscow, RUS, Hard (I): David Nalbandian (ARG) d. Nikolay Davydenko (RUS) 64 76(5) 76(6); Mikhail Youzhny (RUS) d. Leonardo Mayer (ARG) 63 61 64; Eduardo Schwank/Horacio Zeballos (ARG) d. Nikolay Davydenko/Igor Kunitsyn (RUS) 76(7) 64 67(3) 61; Nikolay Davydenko (RUS) d. Eduardo Schwank (ARG) 46 63 61 64; David Nalbandian (ARG) d. Mikhail Youzhny (RUS) 76(5) 64 63.

Serbia defeated Croatia 4-1, Split, CRO, Hard (I): Novak Djokovic (SRB) d. Ivan Ljubicic (CRO) 76(3) 64 61; Marin Cilic (CRO) d. Viktor Troicki (SRB) 64 75 62; Janko Tipsarevic/Nenad Zimonjic (SRB) d. Marin Cilic/Ivan Dodig (CRO) 63 62 64; Novak Djokovic (SRB) d. Marin Cilic (CRO) 63 63 62; Janko Tipsarevic (SRB) d. Antonio Veic (CRO) 62 76(5).

Czech Republic defeated Chile 4-1, Coquimbo, CHI, Clay (O): Ivo Minar (CZE) d. Nicolas Massu (CHI) 60 62 63; Jan Hajek (CZE) d. Paul Capdeville (CHI) 60 62 61; Lukas Dlouhy/Jan Hajek (CZE) d. Jorge Aguilar/Nicolas Massu (CHI) 76(3) 63 36 63; Jorge Aguilar (CHI) d. Lukas Dlouhy (CZE) 61 76(6); Ivo Minar (CZE) d. Cristobal Saavedra-Corvalan (CHI) 76(2) 62.

Semifinals 17-19 September
France defeated Argentina 5-0, Lyon, FRA, Hard (I): Michael Llodra (FRA) d. Juan Monaco (ARG) 75 46 75 63; Gael Monfils (FRA) d. David Nalbandian (ARG) 64 26 64 63; Arnaud Clement/Michael Llodra (FRA) d. Eduardo Schwank/Horacio Zeballos (ARG) 64 75 63; Gilles Simon (FRA) d. Eduardo Schwank (ARG) 76(5) 67(6) 63; Arnaud Clement (FRA) d. Horacio Zeballos (ARG) 75 61.

Serbia defeated Czech Republic 3-2, Belgrade, SRB, Hard (I): Radek Stepanek (CZE) d. Viktor Troicki (SRB) 46 62 64 64; Janko Tipsarevic (SRB) d. Tomas Berdych (CZE) 75 62 26 76(5); Tomas Berdych/Radek Stepanek (CZE) d. Novak Djokovic/Nenad Zimonjic (SRB) 36 61 64 61; Novak Djokovic (SRB) d. Tomas Berdych (CZE) 46 63 62 64; Janko Tipsarevic (SRB) d. Radek Stepanek (CZE) 60 76(6) 64.

Final 3-5 December
Serbia defeated France 3-2, Belgrade, SRB, Hard (I): Gael Monfils (FRA) d. Janko Tipsarevic (SRB) 61 76(4) 60; Novak Djokovic (SRB) d. Gilles Simon (FRA) 63 61 75; Arnaud Clement/Michael Llodra (FRA) d. Viktor Troicki/Nenad Zimonjic (SRB) 36 67(3) 64 75 64; Novak Djokovic (SRB) d. Gael Monfils (FRA) 62 62 64; Viktor Troicki (SRB) d. Michael Llodra (FRA) 62 62 63.

World Group play-offs 17-19 September
Austria defeated Israel 3-2, Tel Aviv, ISR, Hard (I): Dudi Sela (ISR) d. Andreas Haider-Maurer (AUT) 64 61 63; Jurgen Melzer (AUT) d. Harel Levy (ISR) 64 63 63; Jonathan Erlich/Andy Ram (ISR) d. Jurgen Melzer/Alexander Peya (AUT) 76(2) 64 64; Jurgen Melzer (AUT) d. Dudi Sela (ISR) 64 60 63; Martin Fischer (AUT) d. Harel Levy (ISR) 26 63 60 63.

USA defeated Colombia 3-1, Bogota, COL, Clay (O): Mardy Fish (USA) d. Alejandro Falla (COL) 46 61 64 36 64; Santiago Giraldo (COL) d. Sam Querrey (USA) 62 64 75; Mardy Fish/John Isner (USA) d. Robert Farah/Carlos Salamanca (COL) 64 64 67(5) 63; Mardy Fish (USA) d. Santiago Giraldo (COL) 36 63 75 46 86; Carlos Salamanca (COL) v. Ryan Harrison (USA) not played.

Germany defeated South Africa 5-0, Stuttgart, GER, Clay (O): Philipp Kohlschreiber (GER) d. Rik de Voest (RSA) 64 64 64; Florian Mayer (GER) d. Izak van der Merwe (RSA) 63 36 61 76(6); Andreas Beck/Christopher Kas (GER) d. Rik de Voest/Wesley Moodie (RSA) 64 36 63 64; Andreas Beck (GER) d. Izak van der Merwe (RSA) 75 62; Florian Mayer (GER) d. Rik de Voest (RSA) 63 67(8) 62.

Sweden defeated Italy 3-2, Lidkoping, SWE, Hard (I): Potito Starace (ITA) d. Andreas Vinciguerra (SWE) 62 62 62; Robin Soderling (SWE) d. Fabio Fognini (ITA) 61 63 62; Simon Aspelin/Robert Lindstedt (SWE) d. Simone Bolelli/Potito Starace (ITA) 57 67(0) 76(4) 63 75; Robin Soderling (SWE) d. Simone Bolelli (ITA) 63 63 63; Fabio Fognini (ITA) d. Andreas Vinciguerra (SWE) 61 63.

India defeated Brazil 3-2, Chennai, IND, Hard (O): Thomaz Bellucci (BRA) d. Rohan Bopanna (IND) 67(2) 76(7) 75 46 108; Ricardo Mello (BRA) d. Somdev Devvarman (IND) 46 62 67(3) 62 64; Mahesh Bhupathi/Leander Paes (IND) d. Marcelo Melo/Bruno Soares (BRA) 64 76(5) 61; Somdev Devvarman (IND) d. Thomaz Bellucci (BRA) 76(3) 40 ret.; Rohan Bopanna (IND) d. Ricardo Mello (BRA) 63 76(2) 63.

Belgium defeated Australia 3-2, Cairns, AUS, Hard (O): Lleyton Hewitt (AUS) d. Ruben Bemelmans (BEL) 76(4) 75 26 64; Olivier Rochus (BEL) d. Carsten Ball (AUS) 64 64 76(5); Paul Hanley/Lleyton Hewitt (AUS) d. Ruben Bemelmans/Olivier Rochus (BEL) 61 62 64; Olivier Rochus (BEL) d. Peter Luczak (AUS) 76(8) 64 67(0) 76(2); Steve Darcis (BEL) d. Carsten Ball (AUS) 76(4) 63 64.

Kazakhstan defeated Switzerland 5-0, Astana, KAZ, Hard (I): Andrey Golubev (KAZ) d. Marco Chiudinelli (SUI) 64 64 64; Mikhail Kukushkin (KAZ) d. Stanislas Wawrinka (SUI) 36 61 64 16 63; Andrey Golubev/Yuriy Schukin (KAZ) d. Yves Allegro/Stanislas Wawrinka (SUI) 64 63 63; Andrey Golubev (KAZ) d. Michael Lammer (SUI) 63 62; Mikhail Kukushkin (KAZ) d. Marco Chiudinelli (SUI) 62 64.

Romania defeated Ecuador 5-0, Bucharest, ROU, Clay (O): Victor Hanescu (ROU) d. Ivan Endara (ECU) 62 62 62; Adrian Ungur (ROU) d. Giovanni Lapentti (ECU) 67(2) 46 63 64 61; Victor Hanescu/Horia Tecau (ROU) d. Ivan Endara/Giovanni Lapentti (ECU) 62 62 62; Victor Crivoi (ROU) d. Giovanni Lapentti (ECU) 62 64; Adrian Ungur (ROU) d. Emilio Gomez (ECU) 63 64.

GROUP I

Americas Zone
First Round 5-7 March
Uruguay defeated Dominican Republic 4-1, Santo Domingo, DOM, Hard (O): Pablo Cuevas (URU) d. Jose Hernandez (DOM) 62 75 63; Marcel Felder (URU) d. Victor Estrella (DOM) 06 36 64 63 62; Pablo Cuevas/Marcel Felder (URU) d. Victor Estrella/Jhonson Garcia (DOM) 76(2) 76(5) 63; Jhonson Garcia (DOM) d. Martin Cuevas (URU) 61 62; Ariel Behar (URU) d. Jesus Francisco Felix (DOM) 64 67(3) 62.

Second Round 5-7 March
Colombia defeated Canada 4-1, Bogota, COL, Clay (O): Carlos Salamanca (COL) d. Peter Polansky (CAN) 64 63 62; Santiago Giraldo (COL) d. Milos Raonic (CAN) 75 46 64 64; Daniel Nestor/Milos Raonic (CAN) d. Juan-Sebastian Cabal/Alejandro Falla (COL) 76(4) 76(3) 57 63; Santiago Giraldo (COL) d. Steven Diez (CAN) 63 63 63; Juan-Sebastian Cabal (COL) d. Milos Raonic (CAN) 67(6) 63 64.

Brazil defeated Uruguay 5-0, Bauru, BRA, Clay (O): Marcos Daniel (BRA) d. Marcel Felder (URU) 64 61 61; Thomaz Bellucci (BRA) d. Martin Cuevas (URU) 64 63 62; Marcelo Melo/Bruno Soares (BRA) d. Ariel Behar/Marcel Felder (URU) 63 62 76(4); Thomaz Bellucci (BRA) d. Marcel Felder (URU) 64 61; Marcelo Melo (BRA) d. Martin Cuevas (URU) 67(5) 62 75.

Brazil and Colombia advanced to the World Group play-offs on 17-19 September 2010.

Relegation Play-off 17-19 September
Canada defeated Dominican Republic 5-0, Toronto, CAN, Hard (O): Peter Polansky (CAN) d. Jhonson Garcia (DOM) 76(4) 46 63 63; Milos Raonic (CAN) d. Victor Estrella (DOM) 57 62 36 76(3) 97; Frank Dancevic/Daniel Nestor (CAN) d. Victor Estrella/Jhonson Garcia (DOM) 63 64 63; Peter Polansky (CAN) d. Victor Estrella (DOM) 61 62; Frank Dancevic (CAN) d. Luis Delgado (DOM) 61 60.

Dominican Republic relegated to Americas Zone Group II in 2011.

Asia/Oceania Zone
First Round 5-7 March
Australia defeated Chinese Taipei 5-0, Melbourne, AUS, Hard (O): Bernard Tomic (AUS) d. Tsung-Hua Yang (TPE) 62 61 61; Peter Luczak (AUS) d. Chu-Huan Yi (TPE) 46 63 62 63; Carsten Ball/Paul Hanley (AUS) d. Tsung-Hua Yang/Chu-Huan Yi (TPE) 76(4) 76(2) 62; Peter Luczak (AUS) d. Tsung-Hua Yang (TPE) 63 63; Bernard Tomic (AUS) d. Hsin-Han Lee (TPE) 67(4) 60 63.

Japan defeated Philippines 5-0, Osaka, JPN, Carpet (I): Tatsuma Ito (JPN) d. Treat Huey (PHI) 36 63 64 36 64; Go Soeda (JPN) d. Cecil Mamiit (PHI) 67(4) 63 63 63; Toshihide Matsui/Takao Suzuki (JPN) d. Treat Huey/Cecil Mamiit (PHI) 64 64 63; Tatsuma Ito (JPN) d. Cecil Mamiit (PHI) 64 76(4); Go Soeda (JPN) d. Francis Casey Alcantara (PHI) 61 60.

China P.R. defeated Uzbekistan 3-2, Guangdong, CHN, Hard (I): Denis Istomin (UZB) d. Di Wu (CHN) 26 63 75 64; Ze Zhang (CHN) d. Farrukh Dustov (UZB) 64 06 75 63; Mao-Xin Gong/Zhe Li (CHN) d. Farrukh Dustov/Denis Istomin (UZB) 63 63 64; Denis Istomin (UZB) d. Ze Zhang (CHN) 46 75 62 75; Di Wu (CHN) d. Murad Inoyatov (UZB) 36 62 63 63.

Kazakhstan defeated Korea, Rep. 5-0, Astana, KAZ, Clay (I): Andrey Golubev (KAZ) d. Yong-Kyu Lim (KOR) 61 61 64; Mikhail Kukushkin (KAZ) d. Kyu-Tae Im (KOR) 64 76(9) 76(5); Andrey Golubev/Yuriy Schukin (KAZ) d. Hyun-Joon Kim/Jae-Min Seol (KOR) 67(6) 63 62 64; Andrey Golubev (KAZ) d. Hyun-Joon Kim (KOR) 61 61; Mikhail Kukushkin (KAZ) d. Yong-Kyu Lim (KOR) 75 64.

Second Round 7-9 May
Australia defeated Japan 5-0, Brisbane, AUS, Clay (O): Lleyton Hewitt (AUS) d. Tatsuma Ito (JPN) 63 63 62; Carsten Ball (AUS) d. Yuichi Sugita (JPN) 63 64 64; Paul Hanley/ Lleyton Hewitt (AUS) d. Go Soeda/Takao Suzuki (JPN) 75 64 60; Lleyton Hewitt (AUS) d. Yuichi Sugita (JPN) 75 62; Carsten Ball (AUS) d. Tatsuma Ito (JPN) 63 76(7).

Kazakhstan defeated China P.R. 4-1, Wuhan, CHN, Hard (O): Andrey Golubev (KAZ) d. Di Wu (CHN) 57 64 64 64; Mikhail Kukushkin (KAZ) d. Ze Zhang (CHN) 63 62 62; Mao-Xin Gong/Zhe Li (CHN) d. Andrey Golubev/Yuriy Schukin (KAZ) 63 62 ret.; Andrey Golubev (KAZ) d. Ze Zhang (CHN) 62 64 63; Mikhail Kukushkin (KAZ) d. Di Wu (CHN) 63 26 75.

Australia and Kazakhstan advanced to the World Group play-offs on 17-19 September 2010.

First Round Relegation Play-offs 9-11 July
Chinese Taipei defeated Philippines 4-1, Kaohsiung, TPE, Hard (O): Tsung-Hua Yang (TPE) d. Treat Huey (PHI) 63 76(5) 76(5); Cecil Mamiit (PHI) d. Ti Chen (TPE) 36 63 41 ret.; Tsung-Hua Yang/Chu-Huan Yi (TPE) d. Treat Huey/Cecil Mamiit (PHI) 63 75 67(3) 76(6); Tsung-Hua Yang (TPE) d. Cecil Mamiit (PHI) 26 63 62 36 63; Hsin-Han Lee (TPE) d. Ruben Gonzales (PHI) 63 60.

Uzbekistan defeated Korea, Rep. 3-2, Gimcheon, KOR, Hard (I): Denis Istomin (UZB) d. Yong-Kyu Lim (KOR) 46 61 75 62; Farrukh Dustov (UZB) d. Young-Jun Kim (KOR) 67(6) 75 63 63; Murad Inoyatov/Denis Istomin (UZB) d. Hyun-Joon Kim/Young-Jun Kim (KOR) 57 63 63 63; Hyun-Joon Kim (KOR) d. Murad Inoyatov (UZB) 75 61; Yong-Kyu Lim (KOR) d. Vaja Uzakov (UZB) 63 61.

Second Round Relegation Play-off 17-19 September
Philippines defeated Korea, Rep. 3-2, Changwon, KOR, Hard (O): Yong-Kyu Lim (KOR) d. Treat Huey (PHI) 67(8) 62 76(7) 76(4); Suk-Young Jeong (KOR) d. Cecil Mamiit (PHI) 06 16 63 60 62; Treat Huey/Cecil Mamiit (PHI) d. Hyun-Joon Kim/Jae-Min Seol (KOR) 63 64 64; Cecil Mamiit (PHI) d. Yong-Kyu Lim (KOR) 36 46 64 11 ret.; Treat Huey (PHI) d. Suk-Young Jeong (KOR) 75 75 63.

Korea, Rep. relegated to Asia/Oceania Zone Group II in 2011.

Europe/Africa Zone
First Round 5-7 March
Italy defeated Belarus 5-0, Castellaneta Marina, ITA, Clay (O): Potito Starace (ITA) d. Uladzimir Ignatik (BLR) 64 61 62; Fabio Fognini (ITA) d. Alexander Bury (BLR) 62 64 61; Simone Bolelli/Potito Starace (ITA) d. Alexander Bury/Max Mirnyi (BLR) 61 64 62; Simone Bolelli (ITA) d. Uladzimir Ignatik (BLR) 63 63; Filippo Volandri (ITA) d. Andrei Vasilevski (BLR) 76(3) 63.

Finland defeated Poland 3-2, Sopot, POL, Hard (I): Jarkko Nieminen (FIN) d. Michal Przysiezny (POL) 67(5) 76(4) 67(5) 76(7) 64; Lukasz Kubot (POL) d. Henri Kontinen (FIN) 64 62 76(5); Mariusz Fyrstenberg/Marcin Matkowski (POL) d. Henri Kontinen/Jarkko Nieminen (FIN) 64 76(4) 46 63; Jarkko Nieminen (FIN) d. Lukasz Kubot (POL) 64 76(6) 67(4) 75; Henri Kontinen (FIN) d. Michal Przysiezny (POL) 64 36 67(4) 76(4) 75.

Ukraine defeated Latvia 4-1, Dnipropetrovsk, UKR, Hard (I): Illya Marchenko (UKR) d. Andis Juska (LAT) 63 62 64; Sergiy Stakhovsky (UKR) d. Deniss Pavlovs (LAT) 62 63 64; Andis Juska/Deniss Pavlovs (LAT) d. Sergei Bubka/Sergiy Stakhovsky (UKR) 76(4) 63 62; Sergiy Stakhovsky (UKR) d. Andis Juska (LAT) 62 57 64 76(2); Ivan Sergeyev (UKR) d. Karlis Lejnieks (LAT) 64 67(6) 61.

Second Round 5-7 March
Austria defeated Slovak Republic 3-2, Bad Gleichenberg, AUT, Hard (I): Lukas Lacko (SVK) d. Daniel Koellerer (AUT) 26 62 76(5) 63; Jurgen Melzer (AUT) d. Martin Klizan (SVK) 63 63 75; Julian Knowle/Jurgen Melzer (AUT) d. Michal Mertinak/Filip Polasek (SVK) 36 61 63 62; Jurgen Melzer (AUT) d. Lukas Lacko (SVK) 76(2) 75 75; Martin Klizan (SVK) d. Daniel Koellerer (AUT) 62 76(3).

Italy defeated Netherlands 4-1, Zoetermeer, NED, Hard (I): Simone Bolelli (ITA) d. Thiemo de Bakker (NED) 76(5) 76(5) 63; Potito Starace (ITA) d. Robin Haase (NED) 75 63 26 76(2); Simone Bolelli/Potito Starace (ITA) d. Robin Haase/Igor Sijsling (NED) 46 63 76(5) 64; Paolo Lorenzi (ITA) d. Igor Sijsling (NED) 64 63; Robin Haase (NED) d. Daniele Bracciali (ITA) 76(4) 75.

South Africa defeated Finland 5-0, Pretoria, RSA, Hard (O): Izak van der Merwe (RSA) d. Harri Heliovaara (FIN) 63 64 36 63; Rik de Voest (RSA) d. Jarkko Nieminen (FIN) 57 63 62 57 63; Rik de Voest/Wesley Moodie (RSA) d. Harri Heliovaara/Jarkko Nieminen (FIN) 62 63 64; Raven Klaasen (RSA) d. Timo Nieminen (FIN) 63 64; Rik de Voest (RSA) d. Harri Heliovaara (FIN) w/o.

Romania defeated Ukraine 3-1, Bucharest, ROU, Clay (O): Victor Hanescu (ROU) d. Illya Marchenko (UKR) 76(1) 75 64; Sergiy Stakhovsky (UKR) d. Adrian Ungur (ROU) 62 67(3) 75 75; Victor Hanescu/Horia Tecau (ROU) d. Sergei Bubka/Sergiy Stakhovsky (UKR) 64 64 62; Victor Hanescu (ROU) d. Sergiy Stakhovsky (UKR) 64 62 75; Marius Copil (ROU) v. Ivan Sergeyev (UKR) 46 21 unf.

Austria, Italy, Romania and South Africa advanced to the World Group play-offs on 17-19 September 2010.

First Round Relegation Play-off 9-11 July
Netherlands defeated Belarus 4-1, Minsk, BLR, Hard (O): Thiemo de Bakker (NED) d. Andrei Vasilevski (BLR) 62 62 75; Robin Haase (NED) d. Uladzimir Ignatik (BLR) 46 57 63 60 63; Uladzimir Ignatik/Max Mirnyi (BLR) d. Thiemo de Bakker/Igor Sijsling (NED) 57 63 76(6) 46 63; Thiemo de Bakker (NED) d. Uladzimir Ignatik (BLR) 61 76(5) 67(4) 64; Robin Haase (NED) d. Andrei Vasilevski (BLR) 63 64.

Second Round Relegation Play-offs 17-19 September
Slovak Republic defeated Belarus 4-1, Minsk, BLR, Hard (O): Uladzimir Ignatik (BLR) d. Martin Klizan (SVK) 76(9) 62 62; Lukas Lacko (SVK) d. Siarhei Betau (BLR) 60 64 64; Michal Mertinak/Filip Polasek (SVK) d. Uladzimir Ignatik/Max Mirnyi (BLR) 76(5) 76(6) 36 46 64; Lukas Lacko (SVK) d. Uladzimir Ignatik (BLR) 61 36 61 67(7) 64; Martin Klizan (SVK) d. Siarhei Betau (BLR) 76(2) 62.

Poland defeated Latvia 3-2, Riga, LAT, Carpet (I): Michal Przysiezny (POL) d. Andis Juska (LAT) 63 64 64; Ernests Gulbis (LAT) d. Jerzy Janowicz (POL) 64 64 36 62; Mariusz Fyrstenberg/Marcin Matkowski (POL) d. Andis Juska/Deniss Pavlovs (LAT) 63 64 76(4); Ernests Gulbis (LAT) d. Michal Przysiezny (POL) 67(5) 61 62 75; Jerzy Janowicz (POL) d. Karlis Lejnieks (LAT) 75 64 76(3).

Belarus and Latvia relegated to Europe/Africa Zone Group II in 2011.

GROUP II

Americas Zone
First Round 5-7 March
Peru defeated El Salvador 5-0, Lima, PER, Clay (O): Ivan Miranda (PER) d. Rafael Arevalo (ESA) 63 62 75; Mauricio Echazu (PER) d. Marcelo Arevalo (ESA) 26 62 64 36 63; Sergio Galdos/Ivan Miranda (PER) d. Marcelo Arevalo/Rafael Arevalo (ESA) 75 36 67(4) 64 64; Alvaro Raposo de Oliveira (PER) d. Marcelo Arevalo (ESA) 75 63; Sergio Galdos (PER) d. Sebastian Moreno (ESA) 60 60.

Venezuela defeated Bolivia 4-1, La Paz, BOL, Clay (O): Yohny Romero (VEN) d. Federico Zeballos (BOL) 76(10) 62 26 62; Roman Recarte (VEN) d. Mauricio Estivariz (BOL) 64 46 62 06 63; Luis David Martinez/Yohny Romero (VEN) d. Mauricio Estivariz/Federico Zeballos (BOL) 63 63 64; Mauricio Doria-Medina (BOL) d. Luis David Martinez (VEN) 57 64 64; Piero Luisi (VEN) d. Marco-Antonio Rojas (BOL) 67(7) 62 63.

Paraguay defeated Netherlands Antilles 4-1, Lambare, PAR, Clay (O): Diego Galeano (PAR) d. Alexander Blom (AHO) 62 63 46 62; Ramon Delgado (PAR) d. Martijn van Haasteren (AHO) 61 62 61; Paulo Carvallo/Ramon Delgado (PAR) d. Alexander Blom/Martijn van Haasteren (AHO) 63 75 61; Alexander Blom (AHO) d. Paulo Carvallo (PAR) 63 36 64; Nicolas Salama (PAR) d. Claudio Dias Conduto (AHO) 64 61.

Mexico defeated Guatemala 5-0, Mexico City, MEX, Clay (O): Bruno Rodriguez (MEX) d. Julen Uriguen (GUA) 64 60 20 ret.; Cesar Ramirez (MEX) d. Christopher Diaz-Figueroa (GUA) 61 63 61; Luis Diaz-Barriga/Daniel Garza (MEX) d. Manuel Chavez/Christopher Diaz-Figueroa (GUA) 75 63 75; Bruno Rodriguez (MEX) d. Christopher Diaz-Figueroa (GUA) 46 64 75; Cesar Ramirez (MEX) d. Wilfredo Gonzalez (GUA) 61 60.

Second Round 9-11 July
Venezuela defeated Peru 3-1, Maracaibo, VEN, Hard (O): David Souto (VEN) d. Mauricio Echazu (PER) 62 64 75; Ivan Miranda (PER) d. Roman Recarte (VEN) 16 63 63 ret.; Jose de Armas/Piero Luisi (VEN) d. Duilio Beretta/Sergio Galdos (PER) 76(6) 75 64; David Souto (VEN) d. Ivan Miranda (PER) 57 36 62 62 1210; Roman Recarte (VEN) v. Mauricio Echazu (PER) not played.

Mexico defeated Paraguay 4-1, Encarnacion, PAR, Clay (O): Daniel Garza (MEX) d. Gustavo Ramirez (PAR) 61 64 62; Daniel Lopez (PAR) d. Cesar Ramirez (MEX) 76(8) 57 64 76(5); Miguel-Angel Reyes-Varela/Bruno Rodriguez (MEX) d. Diego Galeano/Daniel Lopez (PAR) 61 63 63; Daniel Garza (MEX) d. Daniel Lopez (PAR) 62 62 20 ret.; Cesar Ramirez (MEX) d. Jose Benitez (PAR) 60 46 62.

Third Round 17-19 September
Mexico defeated Venezuela 4-1, Mexico City, MEX, Clay (O): Daniel Garza (MEX) d. Roman Recarte (VEN) 62 62 62; Cesar Ramirez (MEX) d. Jose de Armas (VEN) 61 63 63; Miguel-Angel Reyes-Varela/Bruno Rodriguez (MEX) d. Jose de Armas/Piero Luisi (VEN) 76(2) 63 62; Daniel Garza (MEX) d. Luis David Martinez (VEN) 64 61; Piero Luisi (VEN) d. Cesar Ramirez (MEX) 64 64.

Mexico promoted to Americas Zone Group I in 2011.

Relegation Play-offs 9-11 July
El Salvador defeated Bolivia 4-1, Cochabamba, BOL, Clay (O): Rafael Arevalo (ESA) d. Mauricio Estivariz (BOL) 64 16 46 76(6) 86; Marcelo Arevalo (ESA) d. Mauricio Doria-Medina (BOL) 76(4) 62 76(5); Marcelo Arevalo/Rafael Arevalo (ESA) d. Mauricio Doria-Medina/Federico Zeballos (BOL) 64 64 61; Rodrigo Rappaccioli (ESA) d. Federico Zeballos (BOL) 61 16 76(3); Hugo Dellien (BOL) d. Sebastian Moreno (ESA) 61 75.

Netherlands Antilles defeated Guatemala 3-2, Guatemala City, GUA, Hard (O): Martijn van Haasteren (AHO) d. Christopher Diaz-Figueroa (GUA) 63 76(5) 46 26 62; Julen Uriguen (GUA) d. Alexander Blom (AHO) 67(2) 63 36 64 63; Alexander Blom/Martijn van Haasteren (AHO) d. Manuel Chavez/Sebastien Vidal (GUA) 76(7) 76(3) 63; Alexander Blom (AHO) d. Christopher Diaz-Figueroa (GUA) 76(5) 36 63 64; Sebastien Vidal (GUA) d. Gino Meeuwsen (AHO) 63 63.

Bolivia and Guatemala relegated to Americas Zone Group III in 2011.

Asia/Oceania Zone
First Round 5-7 March
Thailand defeated Pacific Oceania 5-0, Nonthaburi, THA, Hard (O): Perakiat Siriluethaiwattana (THA) d. Michael Leong (POC) 75 61 63; Kittiphong Wachiramanowong (THA) d. Cyril Jacobe (POC) 64 61 60; Sanchai Ratiwatana/Sonchat Ratiwatana (THA) d. Brett Baudinet/Cyril Jacobe (POC) 64 61 63; Kittiphong Wachiramanowong (THA) d. Michael Leong (POC) 62 61; Perakiat Siriluethaiwattana (THA) d. Cyril Jacobe (POC) 75 62.

Indonesia defeated Malaysia 5-0, Kuala Lumpur, MAS, Hard (I): Christopher Rungkat (INA) d. Ariez Elyaas Deen Heshaam (MAS) 60 61 62; Sunu-Wahyu Trijati (INA) d. Yew-Ming Si (MAS) 46 76(5) 62 62; Ketut-Nesa Arta/Christopher Rungkat (INA) d. Adam Jaya/ Yew-Ming Si (MAS) 62 63 36 76(6); David Agung Susanto (INA) d. Mohd Assri Merzuki (MAS) 63 63; Sunu-Wahyu Trijati (INA) d. Ariez Elyaas Deen Heshaam (MAS) 64 63.

Pakistan defeated Hong Kong, China 3-1, Victoria Park, HKG, Hard (O): Hiu-Tung Yu (HKG) d. Aqeel Khan (PAK) 64 62 36 63; Aisam Qureshi (PAK) d. Cheuk-Wai Hui (HKG) 63 63 64; Aqeel Khan/Aisam Qureshi (PAK) d. Cheuk-Wai Hui/Hiu-Tung Yu (HKG) 26 63 64 64; Aisam Qureshi (PAK) d. Hiu-Tung Yu (HKG) 63 64 64; Siu-Fai Kelvin Lam (HKG) v. Yasir Khan (PAK) 21 unf.

New Zealand defeated Sri Lanka 3-2, Colombo, SRI, Clay (O): Jose Statham (NZL) d. Harshana Godamanna (SRI) 64 36 46 63 64; Daniel King-Turner (NZL) d. Rajeev Rajapakse (SRI) 62 36 61 62; Harshana Godamanna/Rajeev Rajapakse (SRI) d. Marcus Daniell/ Daniel King-Turner (NZL) 76(5) 64 63; Harshana Godamanna (SRI) d. Daniel King-Turner (NZL) 46 46 75 76(4) 30 ret.; Jose Statham (NZL) d. Rajeev Rajapakse (SRI) 61 60 75.

Second Round 9-11 July
Thailand defeated Indonesia 4-1, Jakarta, INA, Hard (O): Kittiphong Wachiramanowong (THA) d. Sunu-Wahyu Trijati (INA) 36 75 64 57 62; Christopher Rungkat (INA) d. Weerapat Doakmaiklee (THA) 64 62 60; Sanchai Ratiwatana/Sonchat Ratiwatana (THA) d. Ketut-Nesa Arta/Christopher Rungkat (INA) 67(2) 64 64 63; Kittiphong Wachiramanowong (THA) d. Christopher Rungkat (INA) 46 62 64 64; Weerapat Doakmaiklee (THA) d. David Agung Susanto (INA) 63 64.

New Zealand defeated Pakistan 3-2, Taranaki, NZL, Hard (I): Jose Statham (NZL) d. Aqeel Khan (PAK) 64 60 60; Aisam Qureshi (PAK) d. Michael Venus (NZL) 76(2) 46 62 26 1513; Aqeel Khan/Aisam Qureshi (PAK) d. Marcus Daniell/Michael Venus (NZL) 76(6) 63 62; Jose Statham (NZL) d. Aisam Qureshi (PAK) 62 61 63; Austen Childs (NZL) d. Aqeel Khan (PAK) 61 63 63.

Third Round 17-19 September
New Zealand defeated Thailand 3-2, Nonthaburi, THA, Hard (O): Michael Venus (NZL) d. Weerapat Doakmaiklee (THA) 63 62 76(1); Jose Statham (NZL) d. Kittiphong Wachiramanowong (THA) 46 76(5) 61 76(2); Sanchai Ratiwatana/Sonchat Ratiwatana (THA) d. Daniel King-Turner/Michael Venus (NZL) 06 67(6) 60 63 64; Kittiphong Wachiramanowong (THA) d. Michael Venus (NZL) 75 76(6) 62; Jose Statham (NZL) d. Sanchai Ratiwatana (THA) 61 64 63.

New Zealand promoted to Asia/Oceania Zone Group I in 2011.

Relegation Play-offs 9-11 July
Pacific Oceania defeated Malaysia 3-2, Kuala Lumpur, MAS, Hard (I): Yew-Ming Si (MAS) d. Juan Sebastien Langton (POC) 46 62 36 75 75; Michael Leong (POC) d. Abd-Hazli Bin Zainuddin (MAS) 61 61 60; Cyril Jacobe/Michael Leong (POC) d. Adam Jaya/ Yew-Ming Si (MAS) 76(4) 76(6) 76(2); Michael Leong (POC) d. Ariez Elyaas Deen Heshaam (MAS) 61 60 61; Abd-Hazli Bin Zainuddin (MAS) d. Cyril Jacobe (POC) 75 76(2).

Hong Kong, China defeated Sri Lanka 3-2, Colombo, SRI, Clay (O): Harshana Godamanna (SRI) d. Hiu-Tung Yu (HKG) 63 62 60; Martin Sayer (HKG) d. Dineshkanthan Thangarajah (SRI) 63 62 60; Martin Sayer/Hiu-Tung Yu (HKG) d. Harshana Godamanna/Rajeev Rajapakse (SRI) 64 64 60; Martin Sayer (HKG) d. Harshana Godamanna (SRI) 64 36 63 64; Dineshkanthan Thangarajah (SRI) d. Gilbert Wong (HKG) 63 62.

Malaysia and Sri Lanka relegated to Asia/Oceania Zone Group III in 2011.

Europe/Africa Zone
First Round 5-7 March
Lithuania defeated Great Britain 3-2, Vilnius, LIT, Hard (I): James Ward (GBR) d. Laurynas Grigelis (LTU) 64 62 64; Richard Berankis (LTU) d. Daniel Evans (GBR) 61 46 76(5) 36 63; Colin Fleming/Ken Skupski (GBR) d. Laurynas Grigelis/Dovydas Sakinis (LTU) 60 67(2) 75 63; Richard Berankis (LTU) d. James Ward (GBR) 76(4) 63 64; Laurynas Grigelis (LTU) d. Daniel Evans (GBR) 67(6) 75 60 26 64.

Ireland defeated Turkey 4-1, Dublin, IRL, Carpet (I): James McGee (IRL) d. Haluk Akkoyun (TUR) 62 62 64; Conor Niland (IRL) d. Marsel Ilhan (TUR) 63 62 61; Barry King/James McGee (IRL) d. Haluk Akkoyun/Marsel Ilhan (TUR) 63 61 63; Marsel Ilhan (TUR) d. James McGee (IRL) 62 64; Barry King (IRL) d. Baris Erguden (TUR) 75 36 62.

Bulgaria defeated Monaco 3-2, Sofia, BUL, Hard (I): Benjamin Balleret (MON) d. Todor Enev (BUL) 46 67(1) 75 62 61; Grigor Dimitrov (BUL) d. Thomas Oger (MON) 64 75 63; Grigor Dimitrov/Tzvetan Mihov (BUL) d. Benjamin Balleret/Guillaume Couillard (MON) 75 63 64; Grigor Dimitrov (BUL) d. Benjamin Balleret (MON) 63 63 61; Thomas Oger (MON) d. Tzvetan Mihov (BUL) 61 64.

Slovenia defeated Norway 5-0, Oslo, NOR, Hard (I): Blaz Kavcic (SLO) d. Stian Boretti (NOR) 62 64 62; Grega Zemlja (SLO) d. Erling Tveit (NOR) 62 62 76(2); Luka Gregorc/Grega Zemlja (SLO) d. Stian Boretti/Erling Tveit (NOR) 76(2) 76(5) 75; Luka Gregorc (SLO) d. Fredrik Ask (NOR) 61 63; Aljaz Bedene (SLO) d. Stian Boretti (NOR) 63 62.

Portugal defeated Denmark 4-1, Maia, POR, Clay (I): Rui Machado (POR) d. Frederik Nielsen (DEN) 46 64 60 61; Frederico Gil (POR) d. Martin Pedersen (DEN) 62 76(7) 36 63; Frederico Gil/Leonardo Tavares (POR) d. Frederik Nielsen/Martin Pedersen (DEN) 64 63 61; Pedro Sousa (POR) d. Frederik Nielsen (DEN) 67(3) 61 61; Martin Pedersen (DEN) d. Leonardo Tavares (POR) 75 64.

Cyprus defeated Egypt 3-2, Limassol, CYP, Hard (I): Karim Maamoun (EGY) d. Rares Cuzdriorean (CYP) 63 64 75; Marcos Baghdatis (CYP) d. Sherif Sabry (EGY) 62 61 61; Marcos Baghdatis/Photos Kallias (CYP) d. Karim Maamoun/Sherif Sabry (EGY) 76(7) 75 61; Marcos Baghdatis (CYP) d. Mohamed Safwat (EGY) 61 62 63; Sherif Sabry (EGY) d. Christopher Koutrouzas (CYP) 61 60.

Estonia defeated Hungary 4-1, Tallinn, EST, Hard (I): Adam Kellner (HUN) d. Jaak Poldma (EST) 63 64 64; Jurgen Zopp (EST) d. Kornel Bardoczky (HUN) 76(7) 61 60; Mait Kunnap/Jurgen Zopp (EST) d. Kornel Bardoczky/Marton Fucsovics (HUN) 63 26 75 57 108; Jurgen Zopp (EST) d. Adam Kellner (HUN) 63 76(4) 64; Vladimir Ivanov (EST) d. Marton Fucsovics (HUN) 64 76(5).

Bosnia/Herzegovina defeated FYR Macedonia 3-2, Veles, MKD, Clay (I): Predrag Rusevski (MKD) d. Ismar Gorcic (BIH) 64 62 64; Aldin Setkic (BIH) d. Dimitar Grabuloski (MKD) 61 64 60; Lazar Magdinchev/Predrag Rusevski (MKD) d. Ismar Gorcic/Aldin Setkic (BIH) 64 64 62; Aldin Setkic (BIH) d. Predrag Rusevski (MKD) 16 75 64 62; Ismar Gorcic (BIH) d. Lazar Magdinchev (MKD) 76(5) 61 63.

Second Round 9-11 July
Lithuania defeated Ireland 3-2, Dublin, IRL, Carpet (I): Richard Berankis (LTU) d. James McGee (IRL) 67(2) 64 64 63; Laurynas Grigelis (LTU) d. Conor Niland (IRL) 62 63 61; Richard Berankis/Laurynas Grigelis (LTU) d. James Cluskey/Barry King (IRL) 63 63 64; Conor Niland (IRL) d. Lukas Mugevicius (LTU) 60 62; James McGee (IRL) d. Dovydas Sakinis (LTU) 62 63.

Slovenia defeated Bulgaria 5-0, Otocec, SLO, Clay (O): Grega Zemlja (SLO) d. Todor Enev (BUL) 63 61 26 64; Blaz Kavcic (SLO) d. Grigor Dimitrov (BUL) 16 61 60 63; Luka Gregorc/Grega Zemlja (SLO) d. Grigor Dimitrov/Ivaylo Traykov (BUL) 67(3) 76(2) 76(12) 63; Blaz Rola (SLO) d. Valentin Dimov (BUL) 60 61; Blaz Kavcic (SLO) d. Todor Enev (BUL) 62 61.

Portugal defeated Cyprus 5-0, Cruz Quebrada, POR, Clay (O): Rui Machado (POR) d. Rares Cuzdriorean (CYP) 63 60 63; Frederico Gil (POR) d. Philippos Tsangaridis (CYP) 60 61 ret.; Frederico Gil/Leonardo Tavares (POR) d. Eleftherios Christou/Rares Cuzdriorean (CYP) 62 61 63; Joao Sousa (POR) d. Eleftherios Christou (CYP) 61 60; Rui Machado (POR) d. Sergis Kyratzis (CYP) 62 60.

Bosnia/Herzegovina defeated Estonia 3-2, Tallinn, EST, Clay (O): Jurgen Zopp (EST) d. Ismar Gorcic (BIH) 64 61 62; Aldin Setkic (BIH) d. Vladimir Ivanov (EST) 64 62 63; Mait Kunnap/Jurgen Zopp (EST) d. Ismar Gorcic/Aldin Setkic (BIH) 62 61 61; Aldin Setkic (BIH) d. Jurgen Zopp (EST) 64 64 63; Damir Dzumhur (BIH) d. Vladimir Ivanov (EST) 26 60 62 63.

Third Round 17-19 September
Slovenia defeated Lithuania 3-2, Vilnius, LIT, Hard (I): Richard Berankis (LTU) d. Blaz Kavcic (SLO) 36 62 76(9) 64; Grega Zemlja (SLO) d. Laurynas Grigelis (LTU) 63 76(4) 63; Richard Berankis/Laurynas Grigelis (LTU) d. Luka Gregorc/Grega Zemlja (SLO) 57 46 61 63 63; Grega Zemlja (SLO) d. Richard Berankis (LTU) 76(2) 64 63; Blaz Kavcic (SLO) d. Laurynas Grigelis (LTU) 64 76(4) 76(5).

Portugal defeated Bosnia/Herzegovina 3-2, Cruz Quebrada, POR, Clay (O): Frederico Gil (POR) d. Amer Delic (BIH) 63 64 67(14) 36 97; Aldin Setkic (BIH) d. Rui Machado (POR) 64 63 16 61; Frederico Gil/Leonardo Tavares (POR) d. Amer Delic/Aldin Setkic (BIH) 61 64 46 64; Frederico Gil (POR) d. Aldin Setkic (BIH) 64 63 63; Damir Dzumhur (BIH) d. Joao Sousa (POR) 46 64 61.

Portugal and Slovenia promoted to Europe/Africa Zone Group I in 2011.

Relegation Play-offs 9-11 July
Great Britain defeated Turkey 5-0, Eastbourne, GBR, Grass (O): Jamie Baker (GBR) d. Ergun Zorlu (TUR) 61 64 61; James Ward (GBR) d. Marsel Ilhan (TUR) 62 75 67(0) 61; Colin Fleming/Ken Skupski (GBR) d. Haluk Akkoyun/Ergun Zorlu (TUR) 63 64 64; Jamie Baker (GBR) d. Tuna Altuna (TUR) 63 62; James Ward (GBR) d. Ergun Zorlu (TUR) 61 63.

Monaco defeated Norway 5-0, Roquebrune Cap Martin, MON, Clay (O): Benjamin Balleret (MON) d. Stian Boretti (NOR) 60 63 21 ret.; Thomas Oger (MON) d. Erling Tveit (NOR) 62 76(5); Guillaume Couillard/Thomas Oger (MON) d. Stian Boretti/Erling Tveit (NOR) 16 61 60 64; Benjamin Balleret (MON) d. Fredrik Ask (NOR) 62 67(6) 60; Thomas Oger (MON) d. Adrian Forberg Skogeng (NOR) 61 62.

Denmark defeated Egypt 5-0, Cairo, EGY, Clay (O): Frederik Nielsen (DEN) d. Sherif Sabry (EGY) 26 64 64 16 64; Martin Pedersen (DEN) d. Karim Maamoun (EGY) 76(4) 67(6) 76(3) 61; Thomas Kromann/Frederik Nielsen (DEN) d. Karim Maamoun/Sherif Sabry (EGY) 63 64 76(5); Thomas Kromann (DEN) d. Karim Maamoun (EGY) 64 63; Soren Wedege (DEN) d. Sherif Sabry (EGY) 75 75.

Hungary defeated FYR Macedonia 4-1, Godollo, HUN, Clay (O): Attila Balazs (HUN) d. Predrag Rusevski (MKD) 64 62 64; Dimitar Grabuloski (MKD) d. Adam Kellner (HUN) 16 57 64 64 62; Gyorgy Balazs/Kornel Bardoczky (HUN) d. Tomislav Jotovski/Lazar Magdinchev (MKD) 36 62 26 60 63; Attila Balazs (HUN) d. Dimitar Grabuloski (MKD) 63 61 62; Gyorgy Balazs (HUN) d. Tomislav Jotovski (MKD) 60 61.

FYR Macedonia, Norway and Turkey relegated to Europe Zone Group III in 2011. Egypt relegated to Africa Zone Group III in 2011.

GROUP III

Africa Zone
Date: 5-8 May **Venue:** Marrakech, Morocco **Surface:** Clay (O)
Group A: Cote d'Ivoire, Kenya, Morocco
Group B: Botswana, Congo, Madagascar, Zimbabwe
Group C: Benin, Cameroon, Ghana, Tunisia
Group D: Algeria, Nigeria, Rwanda

Group A
5 May Cote d'Ivoire defeated Kenya 3-0: Terence Nugent (CIV) d. Francis Thuku Mwangi (KEN) 63 62; Valentin Sanon (CIV) d. Gilbert Kibet (KEN) 60 60; Terence Nugent/Valentin Sanon (CIV) d. Gilbert Kibet/Francis Thuku Mwangi (KEN) 62 62.

6 May Morocco defeated Cote d'Ivoire 3-0: Rabie Chaki (MAR) d. Terence Nugent (CIV) 76(3) 63; Reda El Amrani (MAR) d. Valentin Sanon (CIV) 63 76(1); Talal Ouahabi/Mehdi Ziadi (MAR) d. Terence Nugent/Lavry Sylvain N'Yaba (CIV) 62 61.

7 May Morocco defeated Kenya 3-0: Mehdi Ziadi (MAR) d. Dennis Ochieng (KEN) 60 60; Talal Ouahabi (MAR) d. Francis Mwangi (KEN) 60 60; Rabie Chaki/Reda El Amrani (MAR) d. Francis Thuku Mwangi/Yash Rawal (KEN) 60 61.

Final Positions: 1. Morocco, 2. Cote d'Ivoire, 3. Kenya.

Group B
5 May Madagascar defeated Congo 3-0: Erick Counil (MAD) d. Alain Bemba (CGO) 61 60; Jacob Rasolondrazana (MAD) d. Chatrian Gnitou (CGO) 62 61; Thierry Rajaobelina/ Antso Rakotondramanga (MAD) d. Alain Bemba/Chatrian Gnitou (CGO) 60 62.

Zimbabwe defeated Botswana 3-0: Benjamin Lock (ZIM) d. Lefa Ashley Sibanda (BOT) 60 60; Mark Fynn (ZIM) d. Thabiso Mabaka (BOT) 60 60; Mark Fynn/Admire Mushonga (ZIM) d. Bakang Mosinyi/Shingirai Muzondiwa (BOT) 61 61.

6 May Madagascar defeated Zimbabwe 2-1: Thierry Rajaobelina (MAD) d. Admire Mushonga (ZIM) 64 61; Jacob Rasolondrazana (MAD) d. Mark Fynn (ZIM) 64 62; Mark Fynn/Admire Mushonga (ZIM) d. Antso Rakotondramanga/Jacob Rasolondrazana (MAD) 76(2) 46 63.

Botswana defeated Congo 2-1: Lefa Ashley Sibanda (BOT) d. Gildas Leba (CGO) 60 60; Shingirai Muzondiwa (BOT) d. Chatrian Gnitou (CGO) 75 36 63; Alain Bemba/Chatrian Gnitou (CGO) d. Thabiso Mabaka/Bakang Mosinyi (BOT) 75 36 64.

7 May Madagascar defeated Botswana 3-0: Antso Rakotondramanga (MAD) d. Lefa Ashley Sibanda (BOT) 60 61; Erick Counil (MAD) d. Shingirai Muzondiwa (BOT) 60 60; Antso Rakotondramanga/Jacob Rasolondrazana (MAD) d. Thabiso Mabaka/Bakang Mosinyi (BOT) 60 60.

Zimbabwe defeated Congo 3-0: Benjamin Lock (ZIM) d. Evence Kamessa (CGO) 61 60; Mark Fynn (ZIM) d. Chatrian Gnitou (CGO) 62 62; Mark Fynn/Admire Mushonga (ZIM) d. Alain Bemba/Gildas Leba (CGO) 60 61.

Final Positions: 1. Madagascar, 2. Zimbabwe, 3. Botswana, 4. Congo.

Group C
5 May Tunisia defeated Benin 3-0: Haithem Abid (TUN) d. Theophile Segodo (BEN) 61 60; Malek Jaziri (TUN) d. Loic Didavi (BEN) 62 60; Haithem Abid/Malek Jaziri (TUN) d. Marc Houngbo/Christophe Pognon (BEN) 63 62.

Ghana defeated Cameroon 3-0: Mohammed Salifu (GHA) d. Germain Ayinda (CMR) 75 63; Henry Adjei-Darko (GHA) d. Celestin Nkoueleue (CMR) 60 60; Emmanuel Mensah/ Menford Owusu (GHA) d. Augustin Ntouba/Etienne Teboh (CMR) 75 61.

6 May Tunisia defeated Ghana 3-0: Haithem Abid (TUN) d. Mohammed Salifu (GHA) 75 76(8); Malek Jaziri (TUN) d. Henry Adjei-Darko (GHA) 64 75; Ouassim Derbal/Ahmed Triki (TUN) d. Emmanuel Mensah/Menford Owusu (GHA) 63 63.

Benin defeated Cameroon 2-1: Christophe Pognon (BEN) d. Germain Ayinda (CMR) 62 64; Celestin Nkoueleue (CMR) d. Loic Didavi (BEN) 64 06 76(6); Loic Didavi/Theophile Segodo (BEN) d. Augustin Ntouba/Etienne Teboh (CMR) 46 75 61.

7 May Tunisia defeated Cameroon 3-0: Haithem Abid (TUN) d. Augustin Ntouba (CMR) 60 61; Malek Jaziri (TUN) d. Germain Ayinda (CMR) 62 60; Ouassim Derbal/Ahmed Triki (TUN) d. Celestin Nkoueleue/Augustin Ntouba (CMR) 62 63.

Benin defeated Ghana 2-1: Christophe Pognon (BEN) d. Mohammed Salifu (GHA) 76(5) 16 61; Henry Adjei-Darko (GHA) d. Loic Didavi (BEN) 60 60; Loic Didavi/Christophe Pognon (BEN) d. Henry Adjei-Darko/Mohammed Salifu (GHA) 76(3) 67(4) 63.

Final Positions: 1. Tunisia, 2. Benin, 3. Ghana, 4. Cameroon.

Group D
5 May Nigeria defeated Rwanda 3-0: Abdul-Mumin Babalola (NGR) d. Justin Ntaberanwa (RWA) 62 62; Sunday Emmanuel (NGR) d. Olivier Nkunda (RWA) 63 61; Candy Idoko/Lawal Shehu (NGR) d. Dieu-Donne Habiyambere/Olivier Nkunda (RWA) 61 62.

6 May Algeria defeated Nigeria 2-1: Abdul-Mumin Babalola (NGR) d. Abdelhak Hameurlaine (ALG) 36 76(4) 62; Ouassel Hared (ALG) d. Sunday Emmanuel (NGR) 62 64; Ouassel Hared/Slimane Saoudi (ALG) d. Candy Idoko/Lawal Shehu (NGR) 36 75 75.

7 May Algeria defeated Rwanda 3-0: Abdelhak Hameurlaine (ALG) d. Dieu-Donne Habiyambere (RWA) 60 62; Slimane Saoudi (ALG) d. Olivier Nkunda (RWA) 61 61; Ahmed Ouadane/Slimane Saoudi (ALG) d. Mele Bizimana/Olivier Nkunda (RWA) 61 61.

Final Positions: 1. Algeria, 2. Nigeria, 3. Rwanda.

Play-offs for 1st/4th positions:
8 May Morocco defeated Madagascar 2-0: Rabie Chaki (MAR) d. Antso Rakotondramanga (MAD) 61 64; Reda El Amrani (MAR) d. Jacob Rasolondrazana (MAD) 60 61; doubles not played.

Tunisia defeated Algeria 2-0: Haithem Abid (TUN) d. Ouassel Hared (ALG) 63 62; Malek Jaziri (TUN) d. Slimane Saoudi (ALG) 64 62; doubles not played.

Play-offs for 5th/8th positions:
8 May Nigeria defeated Benin 2-1: Christophe Pognon (BEN) d. Abdul-Mumin Babalola (NGR) 75 62; Sunday Emmanuel (NGR) d. Loic Didavi (BEN) 62 62; Candy Idoko/Lawal Shehu (NGR) d. Marc Houngbo/Christophe Pognon (BEN) 63 61.

Zimbabwe defeated Cote d'Ivoire 2-0: Benjamin Lock (ZIM) d. Lavry Sylvain N'Yaba (CIV) 62 63; Mark Fynn (ZIM) d. Terence Nugent (CIV) 46 64 76(8); doubles not played.

Play-offs for 9th/12th positions:
8 May Ghana defeated Rwanda 3-0: Menford Owusu (GHA) d. Dieu-Donne Habiyambere (RWA) 62 57 60; Emmanuel Mensah (GHA) d. Olivier Nkunda (RWA) 62 62; Emmanuel Mensah/Menford Owusu (GHA) d. Mele Bizimana/Justin Ntaberanwa (RWA) 62 62.

Kenya defeated Botswana 3-0: Francis Thuku Mwangi (KEN) d. Thabiso Mabaka (BOT) 63 63; Gilbert Kibet (KEN) d. Shingirai Muzondiwa (BOT) 64 63; Dennis Ochieng/Yash Rawal (KEN) d. Bakang Mosinyi/Lefa Ashley Sibanda (BOT) 64 36 64.

Play-offs for 13th/14th positions:
8 May Cameroon defeated Congo 3-0: Augustin Ntouba (CMR) d. Evence Kamessa (CGO) 61 60; Germain Ayinda (CMR) d. Gildas Leba (CGO) 61 60; Augustin Ntouba/ Etienne Teboh (CMR) d. Alain Bemba/Chatrian Gnitou (CGO) 75 75.

Final Positions: 1=. Morocco, Tunisia, 3=. Algeria, Madagascar, 5=. Nigeria, Zimbabwe, 7=. Benin, Cote d'Ivoire, 9= Ghana, Kenya, 11=, Botswana, Rwanda, 13. Cameroon, 14. Congo.

Morocco and Tunisia promoted to Europe/Africa Zone Group II in 2011.

Americas Zone
Dates: 7-11 July **Venue:** San Juan, Puerto Rico **Surface:** Hard (O)
Group A: Aruba, Bahamas, Jamaica
Group B: Bermuda, Costa Rica, Haiti, Puerto Rico

Group A
7 July Jamaica defeated Aruba 2-1: Clifford Giel (ARU) d. Dominic Pagon (JAM) 36 62 64; Damion Johnson (JAM) d. Gian Hodgson (ARU) 64 64; Damion Johnson/Dominic Pagon (JAM) d. Clifford Giel/Gian Hodgson (ARU) 46 75 75.

8 July Bahamas defeated Aruba 3-0: Devin Mullings (BAH) d. Ricardo Velasquez (ARU) 60 60; Marvin Rolle (BAH) d. Gian Hodgson (ARU) 62 62; Rodney Carey/Justin Lunn (BAH) d. Mitchell De Jong/Ricardo Velasquez (ARU) 62 62.

9 July Bahamas defeated Jamaica 3-0: Devin Mullings (BAH) d. Yussuf Migoko (JAM) 62 61; Marvin Rolle (BAH) d. Damion Johnson (JAM) 76(1) 63; Devin Mullings/Marvin Rolle (BAH) d. Dominic Pagon/Dwayne Pagon (JAM) 64 61.

Final Positions: 1. Bahamas, 2. Jamaica, 3. Aruba.

Group B
7 July Puerto Rico defeated Bermuda 3-0: Eduardo Pavia Suarez (PUR) d. Gavin Manders (BER) 61 62; Alex Llompart (PUR) d. Na'im Azhar (BER) 63 60; Ricardo Gonzalez-Diaz/Jose Perdomo (PUR) d. David Thomas/Neal Towlson (BER) 63 63.

Haiti defeated Costa Rica 2-1: Ignaci Roca (CRC) d. Joel Allen (HAI) 75 63; Olivier Sajous (HAI) d. Pablo Nunez (CRC) 64 64; Joel Allen/Olivier Sajous (HAI) d. Fernando Martinez-Manrique/Ignaci Roca (CRC) 62 61.

8 July Puerto Rico defeated Haiti 2-1: Ricardo Gonzalez-Diaz (PUR) d. Jean Marc Bazanne (HAI) 64 61; Alex Llompart (PUR) d. Olivier Sajous (HAI) 62 64; Joel Allen/Olivier Sajous (HAI) d. Eduardo Pavia Suarez/Jose Perdomo (PUR) 76(1) 76(2).

Costa Rica defeated Bermuda 2-1: Ignaci Roca (CRC) d. David Thomas (BER) 60 61; Gavin Manders (BER) d. Pablo Nunez (CRC) 64 26 64; Fernando Martinez-Manrique/ Ignaci Roca (CRC) d. Na'im Azhar/Gavin Manders (BER) 60 62.

9 July Puerto Rico defeated Costa Rica 3-0: Eduardo Pavia Suarez (PUR) d. Fernando Martinez-Manrique (CRC) 76(5) 76(3); Alex Llompart (PUR) d. Ignaci Roca (CRC) 61 62; Ricardo Gonzalez-Diaz/Jose Perdomo (PUR) d. Fernando Martinez-Manrique/Jose Carlos Hidalgo (CRC) 61 63.

Haiti defeated Bermuda 3-0: Jean Marc Bazanne (HAI) d. Neal Towlson (BER) 26 64 62; Olivier Sajous (HAI) d. Na'im Azhar (BER) 61 61; Joel Allen/Jean Marc Bazanne (HAI) d. Na'im Azhar/David Thomas (BER) 62 62.

Final Positions: 1. Puerto Rico, 2. Costa Rica, 3. Haiti, 4. Bermuda.

Play-offs for 1st/4th positions:
Results carried forward: Puerto Rico defeated Haiti 2-1; Bahamas defeated Jamaica 3-0.

10 July Puerto Rico defeated Jamaica 3-0: Ricardo Gonzalez-Diaz (PUR) d. Dominic Pagon (JAM) 61 62; Alex Llompart (PUR) d. Damion Johnson (JAM) 62 62; Alex Llompart/Jose Perdomo (PUR) d. Damion Johnson/Dominic Pagon (JAM) 60 64.

Haiti defeated Bahamas 3-0: Joel Allen (HAI) d. Devin Mullings (BAH) 63 76(6); Olivier Sajous (HAI) d. Marvin Rolle (BAH) 63 76(9); Joel Allen/Olivier Sajous (HAI) d. Devin Mullings/Marvin Rolle (BAH) 26 64 75.

11 July Puerto Rico defeated Bahamas 3-0: Ricardo Gonzalez-Diaz (PUR) d. Devin Mullings (BAH) 46 61 76(5); Alex Llompart (PUR) d. Marvin Rolle (BAH) 62 61; Eduardo Pavia Suarez/Jose Perdomo (PUR) d. Rodney Carey/Justin Lunn (BAH) 64 62.

Haiti defeated Jamaica 3-0: Jean Marc Bazanne (HAI) d. Dwayne Pagon (JAM) 62 63; Olivier Sajous (HAI) d. Damion Johnson (JAM) 61 62; Jean Marc Bazanne/Nicolas Etienne (HAI) d. Yussuf Migoko/Dwayne Pagon (JAM) 26 75 63.

Play-offs for 5th/7th positions:
Result carried forward: Costa Rica defeated Bermuda 2-1.

10 July Aruba defeated Bermuda 2-1: Gavin Manders (BER) d. Clifford Giel (ARU) 64 62; Gian Hodgson (ARU) d. Na'im Azhar (BER) 61 62; Clifford Giel/Gian Hodgson (ARU) d. Gavin Manders/Neal Towlson (BER) 63 63.

11 July Costa Rica defeated Aruba 2-1: Clifford Giel (ARU) d. Fernando Martinez-Manrique (CRC) 64 06 62; Ignaci Roca (CRC) d. Gian Hodgson (ARU) 63 61; Fernando Martinez-Manrique/Ignaci Roca (CRC) d. Clifford Giel/Gian Hodgson (ARU) 62 63.

Final Positions: 1. Puerto Rico, 2. Haiti, 3. Bahamas, 4. Jamaica, 5. Costa Rica, 6. Aruba, 7. Bermuda.

Haiti and Puerto Rico promoted to Americas Zone Group II in 2011.
Aruba and Bermuda relegated to Americas Zone Group IV in 2011.

Asia/Oceania Zone
Date: 28 April-2 May **Venue:** Tehran, Iran **Surface:** Clay (O)
Group A: Iran, Kuwait, Syria
Group B: Bangladesh, Lebanon, Oman, Vietnam

Group A
28 April Syria defeated Iran 2-1: Romain Radwan (SYR) d. Ashkan Shokoofi (IRI) 36 64 30 ret.; Shahin Khaledan (IRI) d. Issam Tawil (SYR) 76(5) 63; Hayan Maarouf/Majdi Salim (SYR) d. Mohammed Mohazebnia/Ashkan Shokoofi (IRI) 75 76(8).

29 April Syria defeated Kuwait 3-0: Romain Radwan (SYR) d. Ali Al Ghareeb (KUW) 26 63 62; Issam Tawil (SYR) d. Ahmad Rabeea Muhammad (KUW) 61 62; Hayan Maarouf/Majdi Salim (SYR) d. Ali Ismaeel/Mohammad-Khaliq Siddiq (KUW) 36 76(4) 62.

30 April Iran defeated Kuwait 3-0: Shahin Khaledan (IRI) d. Ali Al Ghareeb (KUW) 61 61; Mohammed Mohazebnia (IRI) d. Ali Ismaeel (KUW) 75 75; Mohsen Hossein Zade/Ashkan Shokoofi (IRI) d. Ali Al Ghareeb/Ali Ismaeel (KUW) 61 76(2).

Final Positions: 1. Syria, 2. Iran, 3. Kuwait.

Group B
28 April Oman defeated Bangladesh 2-1: Mohammed Al Nabhani (OMA) d. Shibu Lal (BAN) 63 61; Sree-Amol Roy (BAN) d. Khalid Al Nabhani (OMA) 64 75; Khalid Al Nabhani/Mohammed Al Nabhani (OMA) d. Ranjan Ram/Sree-Amol Roy (BAN) 36 76(1) 62.

Lebanon defeated Vietnam 2-1: Karim Alayly (LIB) d. Minh-Quan Do (VIE) 62 62; Thanh-Trung Hoang (VIE) d. Michael Massih (LIB) 63 61; Karim Alayly/Patrick Chucri (LIB) d. Minh-Quan Do/Quoc-Khanh Le (VIE) 64 76(6).

29 April Lebanon defeated Oman 2-1: Karim Alayly (LIB) d. Mohammed Al Nabhani (OMA) 62 76(6); Khalid Al Nabhani (OMA) d. Michael Massih (LIB) 63 36 63; Karim Alayly/Patrick Chucri (LIB) d. Khalid Al Nabhani/Mohammed Al Nabhani (OMA) 36 76(2) 64.

Vietnam defeated Bangladesh 3-0: Minh-Quan Do (VIE) d. Shibu Lal (BAN) 62 61; Thanh-Trung Hoang (VIE) d. Sree-Amol Roy (BAN) 60 61; Minh-Quan Do/Thanh-Trung Hoang (VIE) d. Mohammed-Alamgir Hossain/Shibu Lal (BAN) 62 64.

30 April Vietnam defeated Oman 3-0: Minh-Quan Do (VIE) d. Mohammed Al Nabhani (OMA) 61 76(3); Thanh-Trung Hoang (VIE) d. Khalid Al Nabhani (OMA) 62 64; Quoc-Khanh Le/Bui-Tri Nguyen (VIE) d. Abdullah Al Balushi/Mohammed Al Nabhani (OMA) 63 53 ret..

Lebanon defeated Bangladesh 2-1: Mohammed-Alamgir Hossain (BAN) d. Antoine Breikeh (LIB) 46 64 62; Karim Alayly (LIB) d. Ranjan Ram (BAN) 60 63; Antoine Breikeh/Michael Massih (LIB) d. Mohammed-Alamgir Hossain/Shibu Lal (BAN) 75 64.

Final Positions: 1. Oman, 2. Vietnam, 3. Lebanon, 4. Bangladesh.

Play-offs for 1st/4th positions:
Results carried forward: Lebanon defeated Vietnam 2-1; Syria defeated Iran 2-1.

1 May Iran defeated Lebanon 2-0: Shahin Khaledan (IRI) d. Patrick Chucri (LIB) 62 62; Mohammed Mohazebnia (IRI) d. Karim Alayly (LIB) 76(2) 46 75; Karim Alayly/Patrick Chucri (LIB) v. Mohsen Hossein Zade/Ashkan Shokoofi (IRI) 22 unf.

Vietnam defeated Syria 2-1: Minh-Quan Do (VIE) d. Romain Radwan (SYR) 36 63 63; Issam Tawil (SYR) d. Thanh-Trung Hoang (VIE) 62 61; Minh-Quan Do/Quoc-Khanh Le (VIE) d. Hayan Maarouf/Majdi Salim (SYR) 76(8) 62.

2 May Syria defeated Lebanon 2-1: Karim Alayly (LIB) d. Romain Radwan (SYR) 64 75; Issam Tawil (SYR) d. Michael Massih (LIB) 62 61; Hayan Maarouf/Majdi Salim (SYR) d. Karim Alayly/Patrick Chucri (LIB) 76(4) 76(2).

Iran defeated Vietnam 2-0: Shahin Khaledan (IRI) d. Minh-Quan Do (VIE) 76(4) 63; Mohammed Mohazebnia (IRI) d. Thanh-Trung Hoang (VIE) 60 62.

Play-offs for 5th/7th positions:
Result carried forward: Oman defeated Bangladesh 2-1.

1 May Kuwait defeated Bangladesh 2-0: Mohammad-Khaliq Siddiq (KUW) d. Ranjan Ram (BAN) 64 61; Ali Al Ghareeb (KUW) d. Shibu Lal (BAN) 76(3) 26 75.

2 May Kuwait defeated Oman 2-0: Ali Al Ghareeb (KUW) d. Mohammed Al Nabhani (OMA) 63 46 64; Ahmad Rabeea Muhammad (KUW) d. Khalid Al Nabhani (OMA) 76(4) 76(5).

Final Positions: 1. Syria, 2. Iran, 3. Vietnam, 4. Lebanon, 5. Kuwait, 6. Oman, 7. Bangladesh.

Iran and Syria promoted to Asia/Oceania Zone Group II in 2011.
Bangladesh and Oman relegated to Asia/Oceania Zone Group IV in 2011.

Europe Zone
Date: 10-15 May **Venue:** Athens, Greece **Surface:** Hard (O)
Group A: Andorra, Georgia, Iceland, Luxembourg, Malta
Group B: Albania, Armenia, Greece, Moldova, Montenegro, San Marino

Group A
10 May Georgia defeated Iceland 3-0: Lado Chikhladze (GEO) d. Raj-Kumar Bonifacius (ISL) 63 63; George Tsivadze (GEO) d. Andri Jonsson (ISL) 64 62; Lado Chikhladze/Irakli Labadze (GEO) d. Andri Jonsson/Leifur Sigurdarson (ISL) 60 62.

Luxembourg defeated Malta 3-0: Mike Scheidweiler (LUX) d. Denzil Agius (MLT) 60 60; Gilles Muller (LUX) d. Matthew Asciak (MLT) 63 62; Gilles Muller/Mike Scheidweiler (LUX) d. Matthew Asciak/Mark Gatt (MLT) 60 60.

11 May Malta defeated Andorra 2-1: Pau Gerbaud-Farras (AND) d. Denzil Agius (MLT) 62 62; Matthew Asciak (MLT) d. Jean-Baptiste Poux-Gautier (AND) 75 65 ret.; Matthew Asciak/Mark Gatt (MLT) d. Jordi Vila-Vila/Hector Hormigo-Herrera (AND) 57 64 64.

Luxembourg defeated Iceland 3-0: Laurent Bram (LUX) d. Raj-Kumar Bonifacius (ISL) 60 63; Gilles Muller (LUX) d. Andri Jonsson (ISL) 60 63; Gilles Muller/Laurent Bram (LUX) d. Andri Jonsson/Leifur Sigurdarson (ISL) 64 62.

12 May Georgia defeated Andorra 2-1: Lado Chikhladze (GEO) d. Pau Gerbaud-Farras (AND) 62 64; Jean-Baptiste Poux-Gautier (AND) d. George Tsivadze (GEO) 64 63; Lado Chikhladze/Irakli Labadze (GEO) d. Pau Gerbaud-Farras/Jordi Vila-Vila (AND) 63 62.

Malta defeated Iceland 2-1: Andri Jonsson (ISL) d. Bradley Callus (MLT) 63 61; Matthew Asciak (MLT) d. Birkir Gunnarsson (ISL) 62 61; Matthew Asciak/Mark Gatt (MLT) d. Andri Jonsson/Leifur Sigurdarson (ISL) 64 26 63.

13 May Luxembourg defeated Georgia 2-1: Lado Chikhladze (GEO) d. Mike Scheidweiler (LUX) 63 64; Gilles Muller (LUX) d. Nodar Itonishvili (GEO) 62 61; Gilles Muller/Mike Scheidweiler (LUX) d. Lado Chikhladze/Irakli Labadze (GEO) 76(4) 61.
Andorra defeated Iceland 2-1: Raj-Kumar Bonifacius (ISL) d. Pau Gerbaud-Farras (AND) 76(2) 63; Jean-Baptiste Poux-Gautier (AND) d. Andri Jonsson (ISL) 76(5) 63; Jean-Baptiste Poux-Gautier/Jordi Vila-Vila (AND) d. Raj-Kumar Bonifacius/Leifur Sigurdarson (ISL) 26 60 64.

14 May Georgia defeated Malta 2-1: Lado Chikhladze (GEO) d. Bradley Callus (MLT) 60 61; Matthew Asciak (MLT) d. George Tsivadze (GEO) 63 64; Lado Chikhladze/Irakli Labadze (GEO) d. Matthew Asciak/Mark Gatt (MLT) 62 64.

Luxembourg defeated Andorra 2-1: Mike Scheidweiler (LUX) d. Pau Gerbaud-Farras (AND) 62 76(3); Gilles Muller (LUX) d. Jean-Baptiste Poux-Gautier (AND) 75 62; Jean-Baptiste Poux-Gautier/Jordi Vila-Vila (AND) d. Laurent Bram/Joe Hatto (LUX) 16 63 64.

Final Positions: 1. Luxembourg, 2. Georgia, 3. Malta, 4. Andorra, 5. Iceland.

Group B
10 May Greece defeated Albania 3-0: Alexandros Jakupovic (GRE) d. Flavio Dece (ALB) 61 62; Theodoros Angelinos (GRE) d. Ferat Istrefi (ALB) 60 61; Konstantinos Economidis/ Charalampos Kapogiannis (GRE) d. Genci Cakciri/Ferat Istrefi (ALB) 61 63.

Moldova defeated San Marino 3-0: Radu Albot (MDA) d. Domenico Vicini (SMR) 60 61; Andrei Gorban (MDA) d. Diego Zonzini (SMR) 61 61; Radu Albot/Roman Borvanov (MDA) d. Domenico Vicini/Diego Zonzini (SMR) 61 61.

Montenegro defeated Armenia 3-0: Daniel Danilovic (MNE) d. Harutyun Sofyan (ARM) 61 62; Goran Tosic (MNE) d. Khachatur Khachatryan (ARM) 62 61; Ljubomir Celebic/ Nemanja Kontic (MNE) d. Khachatur Khachatryan/Harutyun Sofyan (ARM) 61 62.

11 May Greece defeated Montenegro 2-1: Daniel Danilovic (MNE) d. Alexandros Jakupovic (GRE) 46 76(7) 76(4); Theodoros Angelinos (GRE) d. Goran Tosic (MNE) 64 76(5); Konstantinos Economidis/Alexandros Jakupovic (GRE) d. Daniel Danilovic/Goran Tosic (MNE) 63 75.

Moldova defeated Albania 3-0: Radu Albot (MDA) d. Flavio Dece (ALB) 61 62; Andrei Gorban (MDA) d. Ferat Istrefi (ALB) 60 61; Radu Albot/Roman Borvanov (MDA) d. Genci Cakciri/Flavio Dece (ALB) 61 60.

Armenia defeated San Marino 3-0: Harutyun Sofyan (ARM) d. Alberto Brighi (SMR) 64 62; Ashot Gevorgyan (ARM) d. Diego Zonzini (SMR) 62 57 62; Khachatur Khachatryan/ Harutyun Sofyan (ARM) d. Alberto Brighi/Domenico Vicini (SMR) 75 76(5).

12 May Greece defeated San Marino 3-0: Konstantinos Economidis (GRE) d. Alberto Brighi (SMR) 60 60; Theodoros Angelinos (GRE) d. Diego Zonzini (SMR) 62 61; Konstantinos Economidis/Alexandros Jakupovic (GRE) d. Domenico Vicini/Diego Zonzini (SMR) 62 62.

Moldova defeated Armenia 3-0: Roman Borvanov (MDA) d. Ashot Gevorgyan (ARM) 62 62; Radu Albot (MDA) d. Khachatur Khachatryan (ARM) 60 60; Radu Albot/Roman Borvanov (MDA) d. Ashot Gevorgyan/Khachatur Khachatryan (ARM) 63 61.

Montenegro defeated Albania 3-0: Ljubomir Celebic (MNE) d. Martin Hysenbegasi (ALB) 60 61; Nemanja Kontic (MNE) d. Genci Cakciri (ALB) 63 63; Ljubomir Celebic/Nemanja Kontic (MNE) d. Flavio Dece/Ferat Istrefi (ALB) 75 60.

13 May Greece defeated Moldova 2-1: Radu Albot (MDA) d. Alexandros Jakupovic (GRE) 62 64; Theodoros Angelinos (GRE) d. Andrei Gorban (MDA) 62 64; Konstantinos Economidis/ Alexandros Jakupovic (GRE) d. Radu Albot/Roman Borvanov (MDA) 61 26 64.

Montenegro defeated San Marino 3-0: Ljubomir Celebic (MNE) d. Alberto Brighi (SMR) 61 60; Daniel Danilovic (MNE) d. Diego Zonzini (SMR) 60 61; Ljubomir Celebic/Nemanja Kontic (MNE) d. Domenico Vicini/Diego Zonzini (SMR) 63 61.

Armenia defeated Albania 3-0: Harutyun Sofyan (ARM) d. Flavio Dece (ALB) 62 76(2); Ashot Gevorgyan (ARM) d. Ferat Istrefi (ALB) 61 26 75; Khachatur Khachatryan/Harutyun Sofyan (ARM) d. Genci Cakciri/Flavio Dece (ALB) 62 61.

14 May Greece defeated Armenia 3-0: Charalampos Kapogiannis (GRE) d. Ashot Gevorgyan (ARM) 62 63; Konstantinos Economidis (GRE) d. Khachatur Khachatryan (ARM) 60 61; Theodoros Angelinos/Alexandros Jakupovic (GRE) d. Ashot Gevorgyan/ Khachatur Khachatryan (ARM) 64 60.

Moldova defeated Montenegro 2-1: Radu Albot (MDA) d. Daniel Danilovic (MNE) 63 64; Goran Tosic (MNE) d. Andrei Gorban (MDA) 75 46 63; Radu Albot/Roman Borvanov (MDA) d. Daniel Danilovic/Goran Tosic (MNE) 67(3) 64 64.

San Marino defeated Albania 3-0: Domenico Vicini (SMR) d. Flavio Dece (ALB) 61 62; Diego Zonzini (SMR) d. Ferat Istrefi (ALB) 62 64; Alberto Brighi/Diego Zonzini (SMR) d. Genci Cakciri/Martin Hysenbegasi (ALB) 61 62.

Final Positions: 1. Greece, 2. Moldova, 3. Montenegro, 4. Armenia, 5. San Marino, 6. Albania.

Play-offs for 1st/4th positions:
15 May Greece defeated Georgia 2-1: Konstantinos Economidis (GRE) d. Lado Chikhladze (GEO) 67(5) 76(4) 76(4); Theodoros Angelinos (GRE) d. Irakli Labadze (GEO) 76(5) 62; Lado Chikhladze/Irakli Labadze (GEO) d. Konstantinos Economidis/Alexandros Jakupovic (GRE) w/o.

Luxembourg defeated Moldova 2-1: Radu Albot (MDA) d. Mike Scheidweiler (LUX) 63 63; Gilles Muller (LUX) d. Andrei Gorban (MDA) 64 62; Gilles Muller/Mike Scheidweiler (LUX) d. Radu Albot/Roman Borvanov (MDA) 76(4) 63.

Play-off for 5th/6th positions:
15 May Montenegro defeated Malta 3-0: Ljubomir Celebic (MNE) d. Denzil Agius (MLT) 62 62; Daniel Danilovic (MNE) d. Bradley Callus (MLT) 62 61; Ljubomir Celebic/Nemanja Kontic (MNE) d. Matthew Asciak/Bradley Callus (MLT) 75 63.

Play-off for 7th/8th positions:
15 May Armenia defeated Andorra 3-0: Ashot Gevorgyan (ARM) d. Pau Gerbaud-Farras (AND) 62 61; Khachatur Khachatryan (ARM) d. Hector Hormigo-Herrera (AND) 16 76(2) 32 ret.; Khachatur Khachatryan/Harutyun Sofyan (ARM) d. Pau Gerbaud-Farras/Jordi Vila-Vila (AND) w/o.

Play-off for 9th/10th positions:
15 May Iceland defeated San Marino 2-1: Raj-Kumar Bonifacius (ISL) d. Domenico Vicini (SMR) 76(3) 64; Diego Zonzini (SMR) d. Andri Jonsson (ISL) 64 63; Raj-Kumar Bonifacius/ Leifur Sigurdarson (ISL) d. Domenico Vicini/Diego Zonzini (SMR) 67(6) 75 76(5).

Final Positions: 1=. Greece, Luxembourg, 3=. Georgia, Moldova, 5. Montenegro, 6. Malta, 7. Armenia, 8. Andorra, 9. Iceland, 10. San Marino.

Greece and Luxembourg promoted to Europe/Africa Zone Group II in 2011.

GROUP IV

Americas Zone
Date: 29 June-3 July **Venue:** Panama City, Panama **Surface:** Clay (O)

29 June Barbados defeated Trinidad & Tobago 2-1: Anthony Marshall (BAR) d. Yohansey Williams (TRI) 62 61; Haydn Lewis (BAR) d. Joseph Cadogan (TRI) 62 61; Liam Gomez/ Dawoud Kabli (TRI) d. Ryan Moseley/Seannon Williams (BAR) 63 64.

Panama defeated US Virgin Islands 2-1: Kristepher Elien (ISV) d. Chadd Valdes (PAN) 26 62 61; Alberto Gonzalez (PAN) d. Nicholas Bass (ISV) 61 61; Alberto Gonzalez/Juan Miguel Gonzalez (PAN) d. Kristepher Elien/Terrance Eugene Highfield (ISV) 64 75.

30 June Honduras defeated Panama 2-1: Calton Alvarez (HON) d. Juan Miguel Gonzalez (PAN) 63 62; Alberto Gonzalez (PAN) d. Jose Moncada (HON) 75 76(5); Calton Alvarez/ Jose Moncada (HON) d. Juan Miguel Gonzalez/Chadd Valdes (PAN) 62 64.

Trinidad & Tobago defeated US Virgin Islands 2-1: Brian Oldfield (ISV) d. Yohansey Williams (TRI) 76(6) 76(4); Joseph Cadogan (TRI) d. Kristepher Elien (ISV) 76(7) 64; Liam Gomez/Dawoud Kabli (TRI) d. Nicholas Bass/Brian Oldfield (ISV) 64 61.

1 July Barbados defeated US Virgin Islands 3-0: Anthony Marshall (BAR) d. Brian Oldfield (ISV) 62 60; Haydn Lewis (BAR) d. Kristepher Elien (ISV) 61 63; Ryan Moseley/ Seannon Williams (BAR) d. Nicholas Bass/Brian Oldfield (ISV) 63 62.

Honduras defeated Trinidad & Tobago 2-1: Calton Alvarez (HON) d. Yohansey Williams (TRI) 63 63; Joseph Cadogan (TRI) d. Jose Moncada (HON) 26 63 64; Calton Alvarez/Jose Moncada (HON) d. Liam Gomez/Dawoud Kabli (TRI) 62 46 63.

2 July Barbados defeated Honduras 2-1: Anthony Marshall (BAR) d. Jose Moncada (HON) 64 64; Haydn Lewis (BAR) d. Keny Turcios (HON) 62 63; Ricardo Pineda/Keny Turcios (HON) d. Ryan Moseley/Seannon Williams (BAR) 60 63.

Panama defeated Trinidad & Tobago 2-1: Yohansey Williams (TRI) d. Juan Miguel Gonzalez (PAN) 75 26 62; Alberto Gonzalez (PAN) d. Joseph Cadogan (TRI) 63 76(6); Alberto Gonzalez/Juan Miguel Gonzalez (PAN) d. Liam Gomez/Dawoud Kabli (TRI) 63 75.

3 July Barbados defeated Panama 2-1: Alberto Gonzalez (PAN) d. Anthony Marshall (BAR) 64 61; Haydn Lewis (BAR) d. Walner Espinoza (PAN) 75 61; Haydn Lewis/Ryan Moseley (BAR) d. Juan Miguel Gonzalez/Walner Espinoza (PAN) 64 63.

Honduras defeated US Virgin Islands 3-0: Calton Alvarez (HON) d. Brian Oldfield (ISV) 62 64; Jose Moncada (HON) d. Nicholas Bass (ISV) 60 62; Calton Alvarez/Jose Moncada (HON) d. Nicholas Bass/Brian Oldfield (ISV) 61 60.

Final Positions: 1. Barbados, 2. Honduras, 3. Panama, 4. Trinidad & Tobago, 5. US Virgin Islands.

Barbados and Honduras promoted to Americas Zone Group III in 2011.

Asia/Oceania Zone
Date: 19-24 April **Venue:** Amman, Jordan **Surface:** Hard (O)
Group A: Bahrain, Myanmar, Turkmenistan, United Arab Emirates, Yemen
Group B: Iraq, Jordan, Qatar, Singapore

Group A
19 April United Arab Emirates defeated Yemen 3-0: Omar Awadhy (UAE) d. Ahmed Saif (YEM) 60 61; Mahmoud-Nader Al Baloushi (UAE) d. Fahd Thabit (YEM) 60 60; Rashed Obaid Bushaqar/Hamad Abbas Janahi (UAE) d. Momen Hasan/Ahmed Saif (YEM) 62 62.

Myanmar defeated Turkmenistan 3-0: Zaw-Zaw Latt (MYA) d. Aleksandr Ernepesov (TKM) 63 61; Phyo Min Thar (MYA) d. Amankuli Begenjov (TKM) 61 64; Min Min/Phyo Min Thar (MYA) d. Bahtiyar Atabaev/Eziz Davletov (TKM) 61 62.

20 April United Arab Emirates defeated Turkmenistan 3-0: Omar Awadhy (UAE) d. Aleksandr Ernepesov (TKM) 75 62; Hamad Abbas Janahi (UAE) d. Amankuli Begenjov (TKM) 60 62; Mahmoud-Nader Al Baloushi/Omar Awadhy (UAE) d. Bahtiyar Atabaev/Eziz Davletov (TKM) 61 61.

Bahrain defeated Yemen 3-0: Sayed Hazem Almoosawi (BRN) d. Ahmed Saif (YEM) 64 75; Khaled Al Thawadi (BRN) d. Fahd Thabit (YEM) 63 60; Khaled Al Thawadi/Yusuf Ebrahim Ahmed Abdulla Qaed (BRN) d. Momen Hasan/Mohammed Saif (YEM) 61 60.

21 April Myanmar defeated Bahrain 2-1: Zaw-Zaw Latt (MYA) d. Khaled Al Thawadi (BRN) 61 64; Phyo Min Thar (MYA) d. Yusuf Ebrahim Ahmed Abdulla Qaed (BRN) 61 62; Esam Abdulaal/Khaled Al Thawadi (BRN) d. Zaw-Zaw Latt/Min Min (MYA) 63 64.

Turkmenistan defeated Yemen 3-0: Aleksandr Ernepesov (TKM) d. Ahmed Saif (YEM) 60 30 ret.; Eziz Davletov (TKM) d. Momen Hasan (YEM) 63 62; Bahtiyar Atabaev/Eziz Davletov (TKM) d. Ahmed Saif/Fahd Thabit (YEM) 62 67(6) 63.

22 April United Arab Emirates defeated Bahrain 3-0: Mahmoud-Nader Al Baloushi (UAE) d. Khaled Al Thawadi (BRN) 63 63; Hamad Abbas Janahi (UAE) d. Yusuf Ebrahim Ahmed Abdulla Qaed (BRN) 61 60; Omar Awadhy/Hamad Abbas Janahi (UAE) d. Yusuf Ebrahim Ahmed Abdulla Qaed/Sayed Hazem Almoosawi (BRN) 61 61.

Myanmar defeated Yemen 3-0: Zaw-Zaw Latt (MYA) d. Momen Hasan (YEM) 61 60; Aung Kyaw Naing (MYA) d. Mohammed Saif (YEM) 61 64; Min Min/Phyo Min Thar (MYA) d. Momen Hasan/Fahd Thabit (YEM) 64 64.

23 April United Arab Emirates defeated Myanmar 2-1: Omar Awadhy (UAE) d. Zaw-Zaw Latt (MYA) 64 46 63; Hamad Abbas Janahi (UAE) d. Phyo Min Thar (MYA) 60 62; Zaw-Zaw Latt/Phyo Min Thar (MYA) d. Mahmoud-Nader Al Baloushi/Rashed Obaid Bushaqar (UAE) 64 63.

Bahrain defeated Turkmenistan 2-1: Sayed Hazem Almoosawi (BRN) d. Aleksandr Ernepesov (TKM) 63 64; Khaled Al Thawadi (BRN) d. Amankuli Begenjov (TKM) 76(3) 64; Bahtiyar Atabaev/Eziz Davletov (TKM) d. Esam Abdulaal/Khaled Al Thawadi (BRN) 61 64.

Final Positions: 1. United Arab Emirates, 2. Myanmar, 3. Bahrain, 4. Turkmenistan, 5. Yemen.

Group B
19 April Singapore defeated Iraq 3-0: Chee-Jun Leong (SIN) d. Akram M. Abdalkarem Al-Saady (IRQ) 57 75 63; Stanley Armando (SIN) d. Ali Khairi Hashim Al Mayahi (IRQ) 61 62; Abdul Hakim Bin Jamaludin/Chee-Jun Leong (SIN) d. Ahmed Hamzah Abdulhasan/Ali Khairi Hashim Al Mayahi (IRQ) 63 62.

20 April Jordan defeated Qatar 3-0: Ahmed Ibrahim Ahmad Alhadid (JOR) d. Jabor Mohammed Ali Mutawa (QAT) 62 61; Mohammad Al-Aisowi (JOR) d. Mousa Shanan Zayed (QAT) 64 76(2); Fabio Badra/Fawaz El Hourani (JOR) d. Jabor Mohammed Ali Mutawa/Mousa Shanan Zayed (QAT) 64 62.

21 April Jordan defeated Iraq 3-0: Ahmed Ibrahim Ahmad Alhadid (JOR) d. Akram M. Abdalkarem Al-Saady (IRQ) 60 61; Mohammad Al-Aisowi (JOR) d. Ali Khairi Hashim Al Mayahi (IRQ) 61 64; Fabio Badra/Fawaz El Hourani (JOR) d. Ahmed Hamzah Abdulhasan/Ali Khairi Hashim Al Mayahi (IRQ) 61 76(3).

Singapore defeated Qatar 2-1: Chee-Jun Leong (SIN) d. Jabor Mohammed Ali Mutawa (QAT) 63 62; Mousa Shanan Zayed (QAT) d. Stanley Armando (SIN) 63 62; Stanley Armando/Abdul Hakim Bin Jamaludin (SIN) d. Jabor Mohammed Ali Mutawa/Mousa Shanan Zayed (QAT) 63 63.

22 April Qatar defeated Iraq 3-0: Jabor Mohammed Ali Mutawa (QAT) d. Akram M. Abdalkarem Al-Saady (IRQ) 61 64; Mousa Shanan Zayed (QAT) d. Ali Khairi Hashim Al Mayahi (IRQ) 75 62; Jabor Mohammed Ali Mutawa/Mousa Shanan Zayed (QAT) d. Ali Khairi Hashim Al Mayahi/Akram M. Abdalkarem Al-Saady (IRQ) 67(3) 63 76(3).

23 April Jordan defeated Singapore 3-0: Ahmed Ibrahim Ahmad Alhadid (JOR) d. Abdul Hakim Bin Jamaludin (SIN) 63 75; Mohammad Al-Aisowi (JOR) d. Stanley Armando (SIN) 61 76(2); Ahmed Ibrahim Ahmad Alhadid/Fawaz El Hourani (JOR) d. Abdul Hakim Bin Jamaludin/Chee-Jun Leong (SIN) 76(3) 75.

Final Positions: 1. Jordan, 2. Singapore, 3. Qatar, 4. Iraq.

Play-offs for 1st/4th positions:
24 April United Arab Emirates defeated Singapore 2-1: Omar Awadhy (UAE) d. Abdul Hakim Bin Jamaludin (SIN) 63 60; Hamad Abbas Janahi (UAE) d. Stanley Armando (SIN) 67(3) 62 64; Abdul Hakim Bin Jamaludin/Chee-Jun Leong (SIN) d. Mahmoud-Nader Al Baloushi/Rashed Obaid Bushaqar (UAE) 76(4) 76(2).

Myanmar defeated Jordan 2-1: Zaw-Zaw Latt (MYA) d. Ahmed Ibrahim Ahmad Alhadid (JOR) 76(4) 36 62; Mohammad Al-Aisowi (JOR) d. Phyo Min Thar (MYA) 61 46 63; Zaw-Zaw Latt/Phyo Min Thar (MYA) d. Ahmed Ibrahim Ahmad Alhadid/Fawaz El Hourani (JOR) 76(6) 63.

Play-offs for 5th/6th positions:
24 April Bahrain defeated Qatar 2-1: Khaled Al Thawadi (BRN) d. Jabor Mohammed Ali Mutawa (QAT) 60 61; Mousa Shanan Zayed (QAT) d. Yusuf Ebrahim Ahmed Abdulla Qaed (BRN) 63 61; Khaled Al Thawadi/Yusuf Ebrahim Ahmed Abdulla Qaed (BRN) d. Jabor Mohammed Ali Mutawa/Mousa Shanan Zayed (QAT) 76(0) 62.

Play-offs for 7th/8th positions:
Turkmenistan defeated Iraq 3-0: Aleksandr Ernepesov (TKM) d. Hussein Albeer (IRQ) 61 63; Amankuli Begenjov (TKM) d. Ahmed Hamzah Abdulhasan (IRQ) 62 36 63; Amankuli Begenjov/Aleksandr Ernepesov (TKM) d. Ahmed Hamzah Abdulhasan/Ali Khairi Hashim Al Mayahi (IRQ) 62 64.

Final Positions: 1=. Myanmar, United Arab Emirates, 3=. Jordan, Singapore, 5. Bahrain, 6. Qatar, 7. Turkmenistan, 8. Iraq, 9. Yemen.

Myanmar and United Arab Emirates promoted to Asia/Oceania Zone Group III in 2011.

Acknowledgements

As any sportswriter will tell you, nothing beats playing a sport. Writing about it is just the next best thing to do. And covering the 2010 Davis Cup has been one of those wonderful close-second experiences. In a world where financial considerations are assuming far too great an importance, it has been refreshing to get back to a competition where winning is all that matters.

Tennis players don't compete in the Davis Cup because it will improve their bank balances, but because there is no other experience quite like it. As Novak Djokovic said repeatedly, "When you have this opportunity to play for your country and feel the team spirit, it's something you cannot describe with words."

Every player knows that his career will be incomplete if he doesn't win the Davis Cup: one had only to look at Roger Federer's excitable reaction to winning the doubles at the Beijing Olympics to know what representing your country and being part of a team meant to him. That same joyful reaction was evident throughout this Davis Cup year—not just at the final.

Just as the best players in the world cannot win the Davis Cup without the support of their teammates, so the author of a Davis Cup Yearbook cannot do it without the support of his. Therefore, I am indebted first to Emily Forder-White, the original editor who set me forth on this great adventure, and Ed Pearson, the new editor, who ensured that I complete it.

My other thanks go to the rest of the International Tennis Federation team (in alphabetical order): Chris Archer, Emily Bevan, Jo Burnham, Monica Escolar Rojo, Nick Imison, Mitzi Ingram-Evans, and Barbara Travers; and also, for their invaluable help, Nicola Arzani, John Barrett, Chris Bowers, Yevgeny Fediakov, Craig Gabriel, Lee Goodall, Ori Lewis, Marcelo Maller, Enric Molina, Partab Ramchand, Carlos Ramos, Audrey Snell, Dmitry Tursunov, Rodrigo Valdebenito, and all the players and captains of the Davis Cup teams. Special thanks go to Mariola, Chloe, Phoebe, and Elliot for putting up with me, often on holidays, while I scribbled away.

Clive White

Photography Credits

- **Ron Angle** 67 (top left), 84-85, 86, 87, 88
- **Sergio Carmona** 34, 35, 36, 103 (bottom right)
- **Arne Forsell** 37, 38, 39, 40, 46 (top right) 66 (bottom left), 92, 93
- **Robert Ghement** 66 (bottom middle), 98, 99, 103 (top right)
- **Golovanov/Kivrin** 23, 24, 25, 46 (middle left), 47 (bottom right), 50, 51, 52, 53, 82 (bottom right), 83 (middle right)
- **Manuel Gonzalez** 26 (bottom right), 27 (middle and far right), 29 (top right and bottom), 54, 55, 56, 102 (bottom left)
- **Imagellan** 16, 17, 18, 66 (top left), 83 (bottom right), 102 (top left)
- **International Tennis Hall of Fame** 44, 45
- **Nir Keidar** 66 (middle right), 89
- **Sergei Kivrin** 82 (top left), 97
- **Sergio Llamera** 64, 65
- **Daniel Maurer/Zimmer** 41, 42, 43, 102 (bottom right)
- **Mexico Tennis Federation** 101
- **Press Association Images** 26 (top left), 27 (far left), 28, 29 (top left)
- **Saulo Ruiz** 100
- **Marcelo Ruschel** 46 (bottom left), 47 (middle right), 67 (top right) 83 (top right), 94, 95 (except bottom right)
- **Srdjan Stevanovic** endpapers (front and back), 9, 11 (bottom), 14-15, 30, 31, 32, 33, 47 (top), 57, 58, 59, 66 (top right), 67 (bottom left), 68-69, 75, 76, 77, 78, 79, 82 (bottom left), 83 (top left), 103 (top left), 104-105, 106 (bottom), 107 (top), 108 (bottom), 109, 110 (top and bottom), 113 (bottom), 115 (top), 116, 118 (top left), 119 (bottom left)
- **Tennis Australia** 96 (bottom)
- **Paul Zimmer** 5, 6, 11 (top), 12, 19, 20, 21, 22, 46 (top left, bottom right), 47 (bottom left), 48-49, 60, 61, 62, 63, 67 (top middle and bottom right), 70, 71, 72, 73, 74, 80, 81, 83 (bottom left), 102 (top right), 103 (bottom left), 106 (top), 107 (bottom), 108 (top), 110 (middle), 111, 112, 113 (top), 114, 115 (bottom), 118 (except top left), 119 (except bottom left)
- **Zimmer** 82 (top right), 90, 91